THE TRIAL RECORD OF DENMARK VESEY

The Trial Record of
DENMARK VESEY

Introduction by
JOHN OLIVER KILLENS

Beacon Press *Boston*

Introduction by John Oliver Killens copyright © 1970
Library of Congress catalog card number: 70–101322
Simultaneous casebound and paperback editions
Standard Book Number: 8070–5454–2 (casebound)
                      8070–5455–0 (paperback)
Published simultaneously in Canada by Saunders of Toronto, Ltd.
Beacon Press books are published under the auspices
of the Unitarian Universalist Association
Printed in the United States of America

CONTENTS

INTRODUCTION

BY JOHN OLIVER KILLENS

T his is a good book, a valuable book, a most important document, especially for our crucial times. There is something here for almost everybody. More than just a book, it is many books. There is raw material in great abundance here for the historian, the novelist, the artist, the researcher, the dramatist, the poet, and the scholar; the tragedian, the satirist. There is very fertile soil here which has mostly gone uncultivated for the last one hundred and fifty years. Except for notable exceptions like John Lofton's *Insurrection in South Carolina: The Turbulent World of Denmark Vesey,* this rich earth has remained untended; bush and grass and weeds have been encouraged to grow and cover everything, like an uncaretaken cemetery. The story of the Denmark Vesey Conspiracy was long ago consigned to a lonesome graveyard, buried there in the deep deep darkness of our painful nonremembrance. And too many of us would rather not exhume the body and disturb the skeleton. America has told millions and millions of Little White Lies about this portion of her history. Nevertheless, a nation must first face its history before it can transcend it, if it ever can. The publication of this material about our past is like suddenly flinging open the windows to an old deserted mansion filled with cobwebs and ghosts and yesteryear's lies and aged odors. Now we let the sunlight in and the fresh air of the healing truth.

Thomas Wentworth Higginson called the Denmark Vesey

Conspiracy "the most elaborate insurrectionary project ever formed by American slaves. . . . In boldness of conception and thoroughness of origination there is nothing to compare with it."

The august body of South Carolina magistrates who sat in judgment on the Black and desperate plotters of Charleston declared, piously, "Carolina has been rescued from the most horrible catastrophe with which it has been threatened since it has been an independent state." Some have said that Old John Brown of Kansas received his inspiration from the Vesey incident.

This volume contains the record taken by the court and set down by two of the presiding magistrates, Lionel H. Kennedy and Thomas Parker. I should imagine that it is as fair as any account of its kind can possibly be, considering the fact that it was recorded entirely by, and from the point of view of, the men who sat in judgment. Men who were all white and devout believers in Black inferiority, and who were staunch advocates for the cause of Southern slavery.

No matter; the facts as recorded by the magistrates are so powerful and revealing, they transcend and, yes, subvert, the understanding and intentions of the honorable magistrates. The facts, as recorded, when looked back upon today, explode many of the old myths about the good old genteel days of slavery, the idyllic and aristocratic times of benevolent and kindly masters and loyal and contented slaves. It clears the atmosphere which for centuries has pervaded that era of American history with saccharine sentimentality and the queasy honeysuckled smell of sweet magnolias. Slave uprisings and conspiracies blew away illusions like the eyes of hurricanes. Certainly the gentlemen who originally set this all down for posterity did not intend this record as an antislavery document. But Truth has a way sometimes of catching up with Time and History.

And one of the truths we gather from this "undisputed" document is that there were many slaves who were not childlike and simpleminded, were not happy with their bondage which was, of course, ordained forever by the gods. There were even those Blacks who harbored wrath and hostility toward their masters, and had visions of wreaking vengeance and changing the world and their situation in the world. Yes, there were even Black men, slave and free, who plotted wholesale slaughter against all men, women, and children of the paler pigmentation. There was a Black man named Denmark Vesey who was the leader of a conspiracy to kill all of the white people in Charleston, South Carolina, and in the outlying countryside, north, south, east, west. In spite of Magistrates Kennedy and Parker, a story emerges of Black revolutionaries ready to lay their lives on the line for the cause of Black liberation.

For centuries now the mythmakers of the United States, in order to justify slavery in the land of the free and home of the brave (W. E. B. Du Bois called it the land of the thief and the home of the slave), have pictured slavery as a more or less benevolent institution made to order and ordained by God for the civilizing and Christianizing of the savage pagan Blacks, and only incidentally, and as an afterthought, for the ease and wealth and comfort of the paternalistic Great White Fathers. Indeed, many Southern planters and upright patriots and especially outstanding statesmen like the honorable John Caldwell Calhoun argued righteously for the kind of free American institutions that would be all the freer if the free men could own slaves. From the point of view of the slave, it was a peculiar kind of freedom, a freedom to deny freedom to other men and to profit from their bondage.

From Mrs. Stowe's *Uncle Tom's Cabin* (good intentions notwithstanding) to Dixon's *The Clansman* (movie title *Birth of a Nation*) to Margaret Mitchell's *Gone with the Wind* (which has alas come back again) to Styron's *The Confessions of Nat Turner* (intentions of the author terribly suspect), the mythmakers have consistently romanticized American slavery, even those, like Mrs. Stowe, who were devotedly antislavery. But the material of the Vesey document tells a grimly different story.

Picture Charleston, South Carolina, in the first quarter of the nineteenth century. In 1770, Charleston had been the fourth largest city in all of British America, exceeded only by New York, Boston, and Philadelphia. In 1820, it was a prosperous thriving city with 13,652 slaves, 1,475 free men of color, and 11,654 whites. It was bustling with activity and was the social and commercial center of the Carolinas and of a large part of the entire South. According to author John Lofton, Charleston ranked sixth among the urban centers of the nation in the early 1820's.

The South Carolina aristocracy, the great planters, slaveholders, smacked their lips on turtle soup and fine Madeira (slavery was itself a very heady wine), enjoyed their horse races, cockfights, slave auctions, and elegant balls, as they basked complacently in their best of all possible worlds. True, a miserable few indulged their "guilty consciences" with pious professions that slavery was an evil, albeit a necessary evil, and one that harmed the slaver as much as it did the slave. Even more so, since it did such immeasurable injury to the slaver's soul. Of course, fortunately (or unfortunately?) for the slave, he did not possess a soul or conscience. Did he? It was an attitude somewhat like the one your father used to assume when he took the belt to your backside. Remember? "It hurts me, son, more than it does you." But did you ever believe it?

With all this surface complacency, there was a deep and nervous apprehension which sharply contradicted it. The honeysuckled air was filled with talk about the Godless abolitionists and the Missouri Compromise and congressional debates about slavery's constitutionality. Then there was, of course, the presence—the almost omnipresence—of the Black man himself. "Do we really know the African?" the white man must have continually asked himself. "Is he a man, even like ourselves, capable of conspiracy, deceit, revolt, hostility, and revolution?" With revolts and rumors of revolts and conspiracies almost in the air he breathed, the white slaver had to tell himself, "It cannot happen in our state, especially never can it happen in our town, where we have always had a history of racial harmony. Things are quiet in our town. Our niggers are quiescent niggers." It was the kind of deafening quiet which might be compared with the great hush in the Black urban communities of 1967–68, where the buildings themselves seemed to hold their breaths in expectation of a grand explosion, and politicians whistled in the dark and engaged in self-deception. It could not happen in Watts either. And especially it could not happen in Detroit, where the auto workers union was strong and "progressive" and "integrated" and the Black workers were happy, and there were so many Black homeowners with all those middle-class expectations, aspirations. There are many lessons to learn from the tragedy of Denmark Vesey and the patriots who dreamed with him to liberate the nation.

The facts as to Denmark Vesey's birthplace are unclear. In any event, he was fourteen years of age and living in St. Thomas in the Virgin Islands, when he was taken aboard a slave ship by its captain, Joseph Vesey. The ship was bound for Haiti, where the boy was sold to a white planter. Upon Joseph Vesey's return to Haiti, or Santo Domingo, as it was called by the Europeans, the captain had to buy his slave back, since, according to the planter and the King's physician, the boy was subject to epileptic fits. During Denmark's brief stay in Haiti, the French were already sowing the inevitable seeds of revolution through their inhuman treatment of the Blacks in what was then the most prosperous of colonies in the whole "New World." There was plenty of talk among the Blacks of fighting fire with fire and revolution, and Denmark had to hear it. He might have been subject to epileptic fits, but he was neither deaf nor ever dumb or docile.

After sailing on his master's slave ship for a time, where he witnessed a lot of happenings (a slave ship, after all, was not a Sunday-School-pleasure-picnic-cruiser up the Hudson to Bear Mountain), heard a lot of talk, and learned several languages, he settled with his master in 1783 in Charleston, South Carolina. Denmark must have been sixteen years old at the time. He learned the trade of carpentry and was very skilled at it, and in 1800 he bought his freedom with winnings from a lottery. He was an avid reader. He earned the reputation in the town of being a craftsman of great distinction. Notwithstanding, he also earned a reputation among the white people of being a "mighty uppity nigger!"

Denmark's thirst for freedom was not quenched by the purchase of his individual freedom. He dreamed of an end to slavery everywhere. And he was the kind of dreamer whose dreams led him to action. There is a tradition amongst Black folk for that kind of dreamer, one whose dreams do not drug him into idleness. Folk like Harriet Tubman, Nat Turner, Gabriel Prosser, Frederick Douglass, Malcolm X, Martin Luther King come immediately to mind. Vesey could not rest until all of his brothers and sisters were free. He was a patriot of liberation. And there were other considerations that contributed to his patriotism. Even though he was free, his wife and children belonged to their slavemaster. He could see them only at the pleasure and benevolence of the slavemaster. One does not need much imagination to know how this must have rankled a proud sensitive man like Denmark Vesey. For he was a man possessed of the fiercest dignity. If he saw a Black man bow to a white man on the streets of Charleston, he would scold him angrily, and loudly. "You're a man born equal to any other man. How can you degrade yourself by bowing and scraping to another. I will never cringe before the whites!"

He took every opportunity that presented itself to engage in argument with white men on the question of slavery, especially when the conversation could be overheard by Blacks. He was an expert debater and went to great extremes to make white men look stupid in argument with him. It was all a part of his campaign to show Blacks that whites were not superior or invincible, that when you disputed or berated white men the sun still shone, the earth still turned. The white man was not God.

He earned a reputation among Black folk, slave and free, of being totally unafraid of white men. Many Black folk loved him for it. Some others, especially some who were house slaves, and some who were free men, feared him for it. All respected him. Black and white respected him. Finally, in 1818, he began to talk to a few of his Black brethren about the possibility of a slave insurrection. He could no longer contain the fire burning in him. He had to share his dream with others. He, a free Black man, was ready now to risk everything, even life itself, to secure the liberation of his fellow countrymen.

Vesey was a man obsessed with the question of Black Liberation. It was his religion; it was his *raison d'être,* his life's commitment. He had pondered the question many years, had considered many and varied solutions to the "problem." During those times there was a "Back-to-Africa Movement." He had even considered that way out. But when questioned by one of the slaves, he said, "I did not go with Creighton to Africa, because I did not will it. I wanted to stay here and see what I could do for my Black brothers and sisters." And so it came to pass, that in 1821 a few

Black men began to meet at Denmark's home and plot a rebellion in which the whites of Charleston were to be slain by the Black insurgents and the slaves were to be set free. He was asked by more than one of the insurgents, "But what about the children? Shall we kill them too?" And he answered without hesitation, "What's the sense of killing the louse and leaving the nit?"

One by one he began recruitment to the cause. Divulging the plot to others was a hazardous pursuit. If the whites got wind of it, every Black involved could expect to lose his life by hanging. The men he brought initially into the inner circle of the plot proved to be deserving of his confidence. Proud, fearless, mostly literate, skilled craftsmen, every single one of them was fiercely dedicated to the cause of Black liberation. There were only six of them at first, including Vesey. The others were Peter Poyas, Ned and Rolla Bennett, Monday Gell, and Jack Pritchard, the latter known as Gullah Jack. He was a native of Angola in Africa, a physician and a conjurer.

Gullah Jack was a legendary figure in the Charleston area. It was said of him that he possessed supernatural powers and could not be killed by mortal man, and that he could and would endow such powers on other co-conspirators. They went quietly about their work from day to day, some laughing in the faces of white folks, all of them "happy and contented niggers," and each night they plotted revolution under the cover of darkness, in an atmosphere sometimes thick with great distrust, especially as they went about recruiting others. You only needed one informer. Of the first six patriots, only one betrayed the cause. He was Monday Gell, who broke down under severe pressure and became a "friendly" witness for the State. Peter Poyas, the first to be recruited to the cause by his close friend Denmark, cautioned the others against recruiting the house slaves. "Do not mention our plan to those receiving presents of old coats from their masters, for they will surely betray us." Events proved the accuracy of his prophecy.

Ironically, Thomas Bennett, the then "liberal" governor of South Carolina, was one of those benign white men who liked to boast of the undying loyalty of the colored race to the cause of slavery. Nevertheless, two of the original ringleaders, Ned and

Rolla, were his own chattel property. According to the document
of the trial record, Witness Number 2 against Rolla Bennett testified, "I asked him if he could bind his master or kill him; he
laughed at me again." Witness Number 2 had already testified
that he had once cautioned Rolla, "Take care, God says we must
not kill." And Rolla had laughed at him and called him a coward.

The plotting went apace; the recruitment was phenomenal.
At some of the meetings Vesey would exhort them by elaborating
on the Declaration of Independence and the Constitution. He knew
of the debates against slavery in the Congress of the United States
and was especially impressed by the speeches of Senator Rufus
King of New York. When he ran out of these sources, he preached
liberation from the Bible. It was again ironical that, before the
judge passed sentence on "ten of the criminals," he admonished
them: "In addition to the crime of treason, you have, on the present occasion, displayed the vilest ingratitude. It is a melancholy
truth, that those servants in whom was reposed the most unlimited confidence, have been the principal actors in this wicked
scheme. Reared by the hand of kindness, and fostered by a master
who assumed many of the duties of a parent—you have realized
the fable of the Frozen serpent, and attempted to destroy the
bosom that sheltered and protected you." And these words were
spoken by the judge in all sincerity and with a righteous indignation and without the slightest trace of satirical intent. And further, to Denmark Vesey, with enormous piety: "You have moreover committed the grossest impiety: You have perverted the sacred words of God, and attempted to torture them into a sanction
for crimes, at the bare imagination of which, humanity shudders.
Are you incapable of Heavenly influence of that Gospel, all whose
'paths are peace'? It was to reconcile us to our destinies on earth,
and to enable us to discharge with fidelity all our duties, whether
as master or servant, that those inspired precepts were imparted
by Heaven to fallen men—There is no condition of life which is
not embraced by them; and if you had searched them, in the spirit
of truth, you would have discovered instructions peculiarly applicable to yourselves—'Servants (says Paul) be obedient to them
that are your masters according to the flesh, with fear and trembling, in singleness of your heart, as unto Christ; not with eyeserv-

ice as men pleases, but as servants of Christ, doing the will of God from the heart.' " Obviously, Denmark Vesey preached liberation and war against oppression from other sections of the Holy Book and with a different interpretation.

Vesey declared: "He that is not with me, is against me" (Luke 11:23). Meaning any Blacks who got in their path and didn't join them or who informed on them would be wasted along with the whites. He told his followers they were to spare neither women, children, nor preachers; they were to leave no white skin alive. Quoting Joshua 6:21: "And they utterly destroyed all that was in the city, both man and woman, young and old, and ox, and sheep, and ass, with the edge of the sword." Overriding the qualms and protests of the chickenhearted, he quoted Zechariah 14:1–3: "Behold the day of the Lord cometh, and thy spoil shall be divided in the midst of thee. For I will gather all nations against Jerusalem to battle; and the city shall be taken, and the houses rifled, and women ravished." He was profoundly influenced by the Haitian Revolution and held it before his followers as a great example. Once they struck a blow for freedom, he told them, Africa and Haiti would come to their assistance.

Recruitment continued. Money was raised to send recruiters into the countryside to rally the plantation folk. Arms and ammunition were secured. Pikeheads and swords and bayonets and daggers and other weapons were made, surreptitiously, by conspirators who were blacksmiths. There were times when Denmark did no work at all at his trade of carpentry. He spent full time plotting and planning, giving leadership and instructions, exhorting, checking on this, that, and the other detail. He made many recruiting trips into the countryside as far north as South Santee, and southward from Charleston as far as the Euhaws, which is between seventy and eighty miles from the city. Recruitment reached St. John's Parish at the north and to James' and John's Islands to the south and to the west beyond Bacon's Bridge over the Ashley River. Black troops were enlisted far and wide for the War of Liberation. Eventually Denmark's army grew to nine thousand men, by some accounts. It was difficult to determine the actual number of men involved, since, although lists of names and deployment of troops and the logistics of the operation had all

been put down on paper, not a single list fell into the hands of
the authorities. Vesey burned his papers as soon as he heard that
the plot had been discovered.

The day of retribution was set for a summer day, July 14,
1822, which would fall on a Sunday, a day when many of the
white folk would be out of town. Sunday was also selected because
it was a day when Black folk from the country ordinarily came to
town. The fact of their coming to town in great numbers on that
particular day would not arouse undue suspicion. During the
planning stages, locations of all the places where the authorities
kept their arms and ammunition were duly noted by the conspirators. Places like arsenals and guard houses and armories were to
be the first points of attack. Wigs and false whiskers were to be
made of white men's hair and were to be worn by the liberators
on that day of final judgment. Peter was to lead one group to
seize an arsenal and a guard house. Ned was to lead another from
the countryside and from the Neck, and Rolla to lead another,
which, after killing the Governor and the Intendant (Mayor),
would march through the city and take up station at Cannon's
Bridge, and thus prevent whites from Cannonsborough from entering the city. And so forth and so on, the Black troops were to
be deployed; the leaders in command, Batteau, Vesey, Gullah
Jack. All was in readiness. Then one of the conspirators violated
a cardinal rule laid down for the operation by Peter Poyas. One
of the plotters mentioned the plan to one of those "receiving presents of old coats from their masters."

William Paul tried to recruit Peter Prioleau, a "house slave"
in his heart and soul and mind. Peter Prioleau told his master who
notified the City Intendant who called the city council into session that same afternoon. Governor Thomas Bennett was also in
attendance. Questioning of Peter Prioleau and William Paul led
to the arrest of Peter Poyas and Mingo Harth. When brought before the authorities, they handled themselves with such great
composure and even levity that the authorities were completely
disarmed and released them, but kept them under secret surveil-
lance. Meanwhile they intensified their search for more evidence
of the conspiracy, but found nothing. They were thrown completely off the track when Ned Bennett, who had been named by

William Paul, came forward voluntarily and asked to be questioned, "if I am under suspicion."

An interesting aspect of the conspiracy was that most of the ringleaders were members of the African church, under the leadership of Bishop Morris Brown. Much of the conspiratorial activity took place in and around the church. It was believed that Bishop Brown was aware of the plot, and that, while he may not have participated, he wished it well and gave it his blessings. The Bishop, himself, was out of town when the insurrection was supposed to have taken place. He returned of his own free will, was questioned, and released. Historically, the Black Church has always played a key role in the liberation movement.

Another interesting item in this document was the revelation that there had been other conspiracies. Slave rebellions were not unique occurrences amongst these "docile happy people." Denmark Vesey and Nat Turner were not the only instigators of Black insurgency. To quote the Magistrates themselves:

From the first settlement of Carolina, we have been accustomed to these abortive efforts. Under our proprietary government, there was a notorious outlaw by the name of Sebastian; Governor Gibbs issued his proclamation, and the Indians soon entitled themselves to the reward.

In 1730, a plan was conceived against Charleston—They were allowed to assemble, were then taken, and proper examples made. Some years afterwards, what we denominate *the Gullah War,* occurred—This was more general—in St. Paul's Parish they appeared in arms; the greater part were killed, and not more than two or three escaped. In St. John's Parish they were discovered by Major Cordes' faithful driver Peter, and in Charleston, they were also discovered, suppressed and punished. The Negro law of 1740 was enacted in consequence of the last, and has proved our security from that period, notwithstanding the occasional effervescences of insubordination. The history of South Carolina, in this particular, has been the history of every State in the Union.

Blacks handled themselves with such composure when arrested

and questioned that some of the authorities were inclined to believe that the entire "plot" was the figment of an overactive Black imagination. After all the "niggers" in their town were happy. Weren't they?

The Blacks themselves were not dissuaded or disoriented from their plans of action by this first setback, the crack in their wall of secrecy. On the contrary, they decided to move the date of insurrection forward four weeks. The plan of attack as originally outlined was still to be followed. It was to begin at the stroke of midnight on Sunday night, June 16. Strikes all along the line were to be made simultaneously. The Day of Reckoning came and Blacks came into the city from the countryside. They found the city on a "White" alert, with armed white folk everywhere and the militia in evidence and deployed at all the strategic places. It was obvious to the Black leadership that their plot had been discovered and that the whites were ready for them. One of the main keys to the success of the operation was the element of surprise. How else could they seize the armories and arsenals to take the guns and ammunition? Vesey sent word to the Black liberators to depart from the city and await further orders.

Shortly afterwards, spies were sent into the ranks of the conspirators; arrests of suspected Blacks began again; and finally, some of them broke down and told the entire story of the plot to the authorities. As the magnitude of the conspiracy was realized by the authorities the city was thrown into a state of mass hysteria and righteous indignation. The revelations sent shock waves throughout the genteel and idyllic Southland and across the entire nation. The leaders were arrested and tried and hanged. Their conduct at the "trials" did them great honor. Most of them, excepting some like Monday Gell, obeyed Peter Poyas' admonition to the letter. "Do not open your lips! Die silent, as you shall see me do."

The special tribunal sat in session for five and a half weeks and considered charges against 131 Blacks. Thirty-eight were released for the lack of evidence. Of the 93 put on trial, 67 were convicted and 26 were acquitted. But of the 26 "innocents," 11 were deemed so dangerous they were transported out of the state.

Thirty-five, including Vesey, Rolla, Mingo, Gullah, and Peter Poyas were hanged, some of their bodies left dangling for several days for the edification and cultural uplift of the populace. Forty-three were sent into permanent exile.

The story of the Denmark Vesey Conspiracy was also sent into permanent exile. Many of those very few writers who have tried to evaluate, in essays, the meaning of this remarkable moment in American history, have come to it with prejudices and preconceived opinions of what Vesey and his conspirators were all about. William W. Freehling in his *Prelude to Civil War,* 1965, sees Vesey as a powerful unscrupulous man who was given to fits of rage and violence. And he goes so far as to say that Vesey seemed, even to Blacks he could not convince, to be a bloody dictator whose command they could not question. "Conspirators claimed to fear him more than they did their masters—sometimes more than their God." The secret of Vesey's charismatic power according to Freehling, was "his skillful fusion of the high ideals of the Age of Reason with the ruthless savagery of a barbaric chief." Freehling's kind of attitude is certainly nothing new. Surely Napoleon thought and spoke of Toussaint L'Ouverture as a dictator to his people. But Toussaint's own people thought of him as the Great Liberator, as did all of the exploited around the entire world.

Richard Wade, in a feeble attempt to downgrade the Vesey Conspiracy, wrote in the *Journal of Southern History* (May 1964) an article entitled "The Vesey Plot: A Reconsideration":

> For a concerted revolt against slavery was actually less likely in a city than in the countryside. The chances for success anywhere, of course, were never very good, but ordinary circumstances favored a Nat Turner over a Denmark Vesey. The reasons for this are clear. Nowhere, not even in Charleston, did the Blacks have the great numerical superiority that was present on many plantations. . . . And ironically, the urban environment proved inhospitable to conspiracies because it provided a wider latitude to the slave, a measure of independence within bondage, and some relief from the constant surveillance of the master. This comparative freedom

deflected the discontent, leading Negroes to try to exploit their modest advantages rather than organize for desperate measures.

Black writer and historian, Sterling Stuckey, takes sharp issue with Richard Wade in "Remembering Denmark Vesey," *Negro Digest* (February 1966). He points out that oftentimes it is the better educated, the "privileged amongst the exploited," who lead revolts and revolutions. He gives as examples, Gabriel Prosser, a blacksmith working a few miles out of Richmond who led a conspiracy in 1800, and Nat Turner, himself, who was a literate preacher of "recognized intelligence," even from the point of view of white folk. Of course, Richard Wade misunderstands completely the psychology of the enslaved. Give a slave a cruel master, he dreams of a kindly master. Give him a kindly master and he settles for nothing short of total freedom. Let him achieve his own freedom and, like Vesey, he works until he dies for the liberation of his people. Frederick Douglass expressed it this way: "If a slave has a bad master, his ambition is to get a better; when he gets a better, he aspires to have the best; and when he gets the best, he aspires to be his own master." This is certainly the meaning of the lives of Frederick Douglass, Harriet Tubman, Sojourner Truth, Nat Turner, Malcolm X, Paul Robeson, Martin Luther King, Rap Brown, Floyd McKissick, Stokely Carmichael. It is the meaning of Ned and Rolla Bennett, slaves of the kindly Governor Bennett. This is the meaning of freeman Denmark Vesey, enraged, freedom-loving freedom-fighter. As to the question of the plantation vis-à-vis the city, the city is, until today, the place where the biggest loudest Black explosions have occurred, and will occur.

There was, of course, the South Carolina aftermath, the old "backlash"—nineteenth century vintage. There were state legislatures called into frantic session and city councils convened. Harsher laws against Black men, free and slave, were passed. There were people back in those days, even some abolitionists, who thought, as William Styron argues in these days, that incidents of rebellion like those led by Nat Turner and Denmark Vesey set the cause of emancipation back many decades. But in

1845, James Hammond, proslavery advocate, addressing himself to abolitionists, declared, according to John Lofton's *Insurrection in South Carolina*:

> "But if your course was wholly different—If you distilled nectar from your lips and discoursed sweetest music, could you reasonably indulge the hope of accomplishing your object by such means? Nay, supposing that we were convinced, and thought of slavery as you do, at what era of moral suasion do you imagine you could prevail on us to give up a thousand millions of dollars in the value of our slaves, and a thousand millions of dollars more in the depreciation of our lands, in consequence of the want of laborers to cultivate them?"

Understand?

BIBLIOGRAPHIC NOTE

The text of this reprint is taken from a copy owned by Harvard University in which the following handwritten note appears:

S. M. WELD, JR.
HARVARD COLLEGE LIBRARY

Found in the garret of William Pope's house at Hilton Head, on the 9th November, 1861. It was among a number of old pamphlets and newspapers which had apparently been thrown out and forgotten by the owner. All the copies which could be found were destroyed soon after its publication—it was thought a dangerous document for the slaves to see. It was found by me two days after the battle of Port Royal.

S. M. Weld, Jr.
20th January 1862

AN

OFFICIAL REPORT

OF THE

TRIALS OF SUNDRY NEGROES,

CHARGED

with an Attempt to Raise

AN INSURRECTION

IN THE STATE OF SOUTH CAROLINA:

PRECEDED BY AN

INTRODUCTION AND NARRATIVE;

And in an Appendix,

A REPORT OF THE TRIALS OF

FOUR WHITE PERSONS,

ON INDICTMENTS FOR ATTEMPTING TO EXCITE THE SLAVES TO
INSURRECTION.

*Prepared and Published at the request of the Court,
By Lionel H. Kennedy & Thomas Parker,
Members of the Charleston Bar, and the
Presiding Magistrates of the Court*

CHARLESTON

Printed by James R. Schenck, 23 Broad Street

1822

District of South Carolina.

B E IT REMEMBERED, That on the twenty-second day of October, Anno Domino 1822, and in the forty-seventh year of the Independence of the United States of America, Lionel H. Kennedy and Thomas Parker, Esquires, deposited in this office the title of a book, the right whereof they claim as authors and proprietors, in the words following, to wit:

An Official Report of the Trials of Sundry Negroes, charged with an attempt to raise an Insurrection in the state of South Carolina: Preceded by an Introduction and Narrative; and in an Appendix, a Report of the Trials of four White Persons, on indictments for attempting to excite the Slaves to Insurrection. Prepared and published at the request of the Court, by Lionel H. Kennedy and Thomas Parker, Members of the Charleston Bar, and the presiding Magistrates of the Court.

In conformity to the act of Congress of the United States, entitled, "An Act for the encouragement of learning, by securing the copies of maps, charts, and books, to the authors and proprietors of such copies, during the times therein mentioned;" and also, an act entitled, "An Act, supplementary to an Act, entitled, An Act for the encouragement of learning, by securing the copies of maps, charts, and books to the authors and proprietors of such copies, during the times therein mentioned, and extending the benefits thereof to the arts of designing, engraving, and etching historical and other prints."

JAMES DUDLEY, *District Clerk*

WE, the subscribers, who, with Lionel H. Kennedy and Thomas Parker, Esquires, composed the first Court organized for the trial of slaves and other persons of color, charged with attempting to raise an Insurrection, do hereby certify, that the following Introduction, Narrative, and Report were prepared for publication by request, at a meeting of the members of the said Court; that the same were submitted to us individually for our approbation, and that we unanimously approve of and sanction the publication of the same. We further certify, that the Report of the Trials contains the evidence given in each case.

WM. DRAYTON,
NATHL. HEYWARD,
J. R. PRINGLE,
JAS. LEGARE,
ROBERT J. TURNBULL,
HENRY DEAS.

INTRODUCTION

The account published by the authority of the City Council of Charleston, presents the prominent features of the late contemplated insurrection, but it does not profess to be full and complete, and is ingenuously characterized, as furnishing "a very brief abstract of the testimony offered in the cases brought before the Court." As the public had not an opportunity of witnessing these proceedings in consequence of the peculiar nature of the investigations, which occupied the attention of the Court, and as a very general desire has been expressed to be informed of the details of the plot, as far as it has been developed, the presiding magistrates of the first Court, in whose possession are all the original documents, at the request and under the sanction of the whole Court, have undertaken the present publication. The whole evidence has been given, in each particular case, in the order of its trial, and wherever any additional, or incidental testimony has been disclosed against any criminal subsequent to his conviction, sentence, or execution, it has been duly noticed. The evidence is in most cases preserved, as it was originally taken, without even changing the phraseology, which was generally in the very words used by the witnesses.

Although a different style might have been more agreeable to the ear, it was supposed that this report would be considered more authentic and satisfactory if this method were adopted. It will be perceived, in several instances, that hearsay communications have been recorded, and it may be imagined that they had some influence on the minds of the Court. Such communications were only ad-

1

mitted under the belief that they might lead to further discoveries, but they had no effect whatever on the decision of the cases; and being preserved, it was thought advisable to lay before the public the whole narrative, as it was given by the witnesses, *and not to suppress any part of it.*

It frequently happened in the investigation of this plot, that information was communicated which, as it did not involve the guilt or innocence of any of the criminals, was not recorded; but which, in conjunction with various facts and anecdotes, not committed to writing and within the knowledge perhaps of the Court alone, would be very interesting to the community. In addition, therefore, to a mere report of the trials, and at the suggestion of many, an historical account of the intended insurrection embracing all such information is inserted in this publication under a separate article. On Tuesday, the 18th of June, the Intendant of Charleston informed the authors that there were several colored persons in confinement, charged with an attempt "to excite an insurrection among the blacks against the whites," and requested them to take the necessary steps to organize a Court for the trial of those criminals. The Intendant, at the same time, suggested the names of five gentlemen as freeholders who, possessing in an eminent degree the confidence of the community, and being highly approved of, were immediately summoned, in the form prescribed by law, to assemble the next day, at twelve o'clock. The freeholders convened at the time and place appointed, when the following oath, contained in the act "for the better ordering and governing of Negroes and other slaves," was first administered by the Justices to each other, and then to each freeholder: "You do solemnly swear in the presence of Almighty God, that you will truly and impartially, try and adjudge the prisoners who shall be brought before you upon their trials, and honestly and duly, on your part, put in execution, on these trials, an act, entitled an act for the better ordering and governing of Negroes and other slaves in this state, according to the best of your skill and knowledge. So help you God." After the Court had been thus organized, the Intendant briefly related the circumstances, which led to the detection of the plot, and the preliminary measures adopted, which are detailed in the account published by the authority of the City Council. He at the same time presented to the Court a calendar, containing the names of all the criminals then ascertained, the charges on which they had been committed, and the witnesses against them. Before the Court proceeded to any trial, they were engaged some time in examining all the testimony they could obtain, in order to ascertain how far a conspiracy had really been formed; being convinced by these means of the existence of a plot, they laid down the rules and principles on which the trials should be conducted. As the Court had been organized under a statute of a peculiar and local character, and intended for the government of a distinct class of persons in the community, they were bound to conform their proceedings to its provisions, which depart in many essential features, from the principles of the common law, and some of the settled rules of evidence. The Court, however, determined to adopt those rules, whenever they were not repugnant to, nor expressly excepted by that statute, nor inconsistent with the local situation and policy of the state; and laid down for their own government the following regulations: First—That no slave should be tried, except in the presence of his owner, or his counsel, and that notice should be given, in every case, at least one day before the trial; Second—That the testimony of one witness, unsupported by additional evidence, or by circumstances, should lead to no conviction of a *capital* nature; Third—That the witnesses should be confronted with the accused, and with each other, in every case, except where testimony was given under a solemn pledge that the names of the witnesses should not be divulged, as they declared in some instances, that they apprehended being murdered by the blacks, if it was known that they had volunteered their evidence; Fourth—That the prisoners might be represented by counsel, whenever this was requested by the owners of the slaves, or by the prisoners themselves, if free; Fifth —That the statements or defences of the accused should be heard, in every case, and they be permitted themselves to examine any witness they thought proper.

The Court, on mature deliberation, determined that the public generally, or in other words those, who had no particular interest in the slaves accused, should not be present at their trials; but that the owners of all the slaves tried, and their counsel, as well as the owners of those who were used as witnesses, should be admitted, if they desired it. The Court also extended the same permission to the Intendant and Wardens of Charleston. Among other reasons, which induced this course, were the following: because several witnesses had volunteered their testimony under a solemn pledge of secrecy, and because the further detection of the plot would be greatly impeded, if not entirely stopped, by the accused being apprised of the information against them, and being thus enabled to effect their escape before they could be apprehended.

It was also morally certain, that no colored witness would have ventured to incur the resentment of his comrades by voluntarily disclosing his testimony in a public court. The Court was likewise anxious to prevent the public mind from being excited by the exaggerated representations of the testimony which might have been circulated by auditors under the influence of misapprehension or terror. In the progress of these trials, the propriety of these measures was completely verified, and they were also sanctioned by precedent, on a former occasion, under similar circumstances, at Camden, in this state.

In the conspiracy of the blacks, at Antigua, in 1736, the criminals were tried privately and not even their owners admitted; and in the Negro plot, at the city of New York, in 1741, the trials were in general conducted in a private manner.

After the execution of the first six criminals, and the conviction and passing sentence on five more, two of the latter made disclosures, which caused the arrest of such considerable numbers, that the Court were induced to lay down certain rules of discrimination, in the guilt of the parties, and to adopt two classes of offences. Under the first class were included those who attended the meetings at Denmark Vesey's, at Bulkley's Farm, or at appointed meetings in Monday Gell's shop, for the purpose of obtaining and communicating intelligence of the progress of the conspiracy; all those who aided and abetted in the contribution of money, arms, or ammunition; all those who persuaded others to join; all those who were employed as couriers, to communicate intelligence, or convey orders; and generally, those, who, from their acts or declarations, indicated a hearty concurrence in the plot; and all those, who, after the condemnation of the first six, endeavored to keep up the spirit of insurrection, to promote, or endeavored to promote or excite a party to rescue the prisoners to be executed. Those who were embraced in this class were, upon conviction, to be punished with death. Under the second class were included those who had merely consented to join in the plot, without taking any active part. Those who were included under this class were to be transported beyond the limits of the United States, not to return therein, under the penalty of death.

As the Act of the Legislature, under which the Court were organized, may not be generally known abroad, it is deemed advisable to extract not only such parts of it, as relate immediately to these trials, but so much thereof as may exhibit its general outlines. With this view the following sections are inserted:

9. And whereas natural justice forbids, that any person of what condition soever should be condemned unheard, and the order of civil government requires, that for the due and equal administration of justice, some convenient method and form of trial should be established, *be it therefore enacted,* that all crimes and offences which shall be committed by slaves in this Province, and for which capital punishments shall or lawfully may be inflicted, shall be heard, examined, tried, adjudged, and finally determined by any two Justices assigned to keep the peace, and any number of freeholders not less than three or more than five, in the county where the offence shall be committed, and can be most conveniently assembled; either of which Justices, on complaint made, or information received of any such offence committed by a slave, shall commit the offender to the safe custody of the Constable of the Parish where such offence shall be committed, and shall without delay, by warrant under his hand and seal, call to his assistance, and request any one of the nearest Justices of the Peace, to associate with him; and shall by the same warrant summon such a number of the neighboring freeholders as aforesaid, to assemble and meet together with the said Justices, at a certain day and place not exceeding three days after the apprehending of such slave or slaves; and the Justices and freeholders being so assembled, shall cause the slave accused or charged, to be brought before them, and shall hear the accusation which shall be brought against such slave, and his or her defence, and shall proceed to the examination of witnesses and other evidence, and shall finally hear and determine

the matter brought before them in the most summary and expeditious manner; and in case the offender shall be convicted of any crime, for which by law the offender ought to suffer death, the said Justices shall give judgment, and award and cause execution of their sentence to be done, by inflicting such manner of death, and at such time as the said Justices, by and with the consent of the freeholders, shall direct, and which they shall judge will be most effectual to deter others from offending in the like manner.

10. If any crime or offence, not capital, shall be committed by any slave, such slave shall be proceeded against and tried for such offence, in the manner hereinbefore directed, by any one Justice of the Peace, and any two freeholders of the county where the offence shall be committed, and can be most conveniently assembled; and the said Justice and freeholders shall be summoned, assembled, and called together, and shall proceed upon the trial of any slave who shall commit any offence, not capital, in like manner as is hereinbefore directed for the trying of capital cases. And in case any slave shall be convicted before them of any offence not capital, the said one Justice, by and with the consent of the said freeholders, shall give judgment, for the inflicting of any corporal punishment, not extending to the taking away of life or member, as he and they, in their discretion shall think fit; and shall award and cause execution to be done accordingly. *Provided,* that if the said one Justice and two freeholders, upon examination of any slave charged or accused before them, for an offence not capital, shall find the same to be a greater offence, and may deserve death, they shall with all convenient speed, summons and request the assistance of another Justice, and one or more freeholders, not exceeding three; which said Justice and freeholders newly assembled, shall join with the Justice and freeholders first assembled, and shall proceed in the trial, and unto final judgment and execution, if the case shall so require, in manner as is hereinabove directed for the trial of capital offences.

11. *And be it further enacted,* that two Justices and one freeholder, or one Justice and two freeholders of the said two Justices and three freeholders, shall make a *Quorum,* and the conviction or acquittal of any slave or slaves by such a *Quorum* of them, shall be final in all capital cases; but on the trial of slaves for offences

not capital, it shall and may be sufficient, if before sentence or judgment shall be given, for inflicting a corporal punishment not extending to life or member, that one Justice and any one of the freeholders shall agree, that the slave accused is guilty of the offence with which he shall be charged.

12. So soon as the Justice or Justices and freeholders shall be assembled as aforesaid, in pursuance of the direction of this act, the said Justices shall administer to each other the following oath:

I, ———— do solemnly swear in the presence of Almighty God, That I will truly and impartially try and adjudge the prisoner or prisoners who shall be brought before me, upon his or their trial, and honestly and duly, on my part, put in execution on this trial an act, entitled, An act for the better ordering and governing of Negroes and other slaves in this province, *according to the best of my skill and knowledge,* so help me God.

And the said Justice or Justices having taken the aforesaid oath, shall immediately administer the said oath to every freeholder who shall be assembled as aforesaid, and shall forwith proceed upon the trial of such slave or slaves as shall be brought before them.

13. And for preventing the concealment of crimes and offences committed by slaves, and for the more effectual discovery and bringing slaves to condign punishment, *be it enacted,* that not only the evidence of all free Indians without oath, but the evidence of any slave without oath shall be allowed and admitted, in all cases whatsoever, for or against another slave accused of any crime or offence whatsoever, the weight of which evidence being seriously considered, and compared with all other circumstances attending the case, shall be left to the conscience of the Justices and freeholders.

14. And whereas slaves may be harbored and encouraged to commit offences, and concealed and received by free Negroes; and such free Negroes may escape the punishment due to their crimes, for want of sufficient and legal evidence against them, *be it enacted,* that the evidence of any free Indian or slave without oath, shall

in like manner be allowed and admitted in all cases, against any free Negroes, Indians (free Indians in amity with this government only excepted), mulatto, or mestizo, and all crimes and offences committed by free Negroes, Indians (except as before excepted), mulattoes or mestizos, shall be proceeded in, heard, tried, adjudged, and determined by the Justices and freeholders appointed by this act for the trial of slaves, in like manner, order and form as is hereby directed and appointed for the proceedings and trials of crimes and offences committed by slaves, any law, statute, usage, or custom to the contrary notwithstanding.

15. If any slave in this Province shall commit any crime or offence whatsoever, which by the laws of England, or of this Province, now in force, is or has been made felony without benefit of the clergy, and for which the offender by law ought to suffer death; every such slave, being duly convicted according to the directions of this act, shall suffer death, to be inflicted in such manner as the Justices, by and with the advice and consent of the freeholders, who shall give judgment on the conviction of such slave, shall direct and appoint.

17. Any slave who shall be guilty of homicide of any sort, upon any white person, except by misadventure, or in defence of his master or other person under whose care and government such slave shall be, shall upon conviction thereof as aforesaid, suffer death. And every slave who shall raise or attempt to raise an insurrection in this Province [or shall endeavor to delude or entice any slave to run away and leave this Province],[1] every such slave and slaves, and his and their accomplices, aiders and abettors, shall upon conviction as aforesaid, suffer death. *Provided always,* that it shall and may be lawful to and for the Justices who shall pronounce sentence against such slaves, by and with the advice and consent of the freeholders as aforesaid, if several slaves shall receive sentence at one time, to mitigate and alter the sentence of any slave, other than such as shall be convicted of the homicide of a white person, who they shall think may deserve mercy, and may inflict such corporal punishment (other than death) on any such slave, as they in their discretion shall think fit, anything herein contained to the contrary thereof in any wise notwithstanding.

Provided, that one or more of the said slaves who shall be convicted of the crimes or offences aforesaid, where several are concerned, shall be executed for example, to deter others from offending in the like kind.

18. And to the end that owners of slaves may not be tempted
to conceal the crimes of their slaves, to the prejudice of the public,
be it enacted, that in case any slave shall be put to death, in pursuance of the sentence of the Justices and freeholders aforesaid
(except slaves guilty of murder, and slaves taken in actual rebellion), the said Justices, or one of them, with the advice and consent
of any two of the freeholders, shall, before they award and order
their sentence to be executed, appraise and value the said Negroes
to be put to death, at any sum not exceeding £200 current money,
and shall certify such appraisement to the public treasurer of this
Province, who is hereby authorized and required to pay the same;
one moiety thereof at least to the owner of such slave, or to his
order, and the other moiety, or such part thereof as such Justices
and freeholders shall direct, to the person injured by such offence
for which such slave shall suffer death.

19. And the said Justices, or any of them, are hereby authorized, empowered, and required to summons and compel all persons
whatsoever, to appear and to give evidence upon the trial of any
slave; and if any person shall neglect or refuse to appear, or appearing, shall refuse to give evidence; or if any master or other
person who has the care and government of any slave, shall prevent or hinder any slave under his charge or government from appearing or giving evidence in any matter depending before the
Justices and freeholders aforesaid; the said Justices may, and they
are hereby fully empowered and required to bind every such person offending as aforesaid, by recognizance, with one or more sufficient sureties, to appear at the next general sessions, to answer
such their offences and contempt; and for default of finding sureties, to commit such offender to prison.

53. This act and all clauses therein contained, shall be con-
strued most largely and beneficially for the promoting and carrying into execution this act, and for the encouragement and justification of all persons to be employed in the execution thereof, and

no record, warrant, precept, or commitment to be made by virtue of this act, or the proceedings thereupon, shall be reversed, avoided, or in any ways impeached by reason of any default in form.

A NARRATIVE

OF THE

CONSPIRACY AND INTENDED INSURRECTION,

AMONGST A PORTION OF THE

NEGROES IN THE STATE OF SOUTH CAROLINA,

In the Year 1822.

At the head of this conspiracy stood Denmark Vesey, a free Negro; with him the idea undoubtedly originated. For several years before he disclosed his intentions to anyone, he appears to have been constantly and assiduously engaged in endeavoring to embitter the minds of the colored population against the white. He rendered himself perfectly familiar with all those parts of the Scriptures which he thought he could pervert to his purpose, and would readily quote them to prove that slavery was contrary to the laws of God, that slaves were bound to attempt their emancipation, however shocking and bloody might be the consequences, and that such efforts would not only be pleasing to the Almighty, but were absolutely enjoined, and their success predicted in the Scriptures. His favorite texts when he addressed his own color were, Zechariah, chapter 14, verses 1, 2, and 3,[2] and Joshua, chapter 4, verse 21;[3] and in all his conversations he identified their situation with that of the Israelites. The number of inflammatory pamphlets on slavery brought into Charleston from some of our sister states, within the last four years[4] (and one from Sierra Leone), and distributed among the colored population of the city, for which there was a great facility, in consequence of the unrestricted intercourse allowed to persons of color between the different States in the Union; and the speeches in Congress of those opposed to the admission of Missouri into the Union, perhaps garbled and misrepresented, furnished him with ample means for inflaming the minds of the colored population of this state; and by distorting certain parts of those speeches, or selecting from them particular passages, he persuaded but too many that Congress had actually declared them free, and that they were held in bondage contrary to the laws of the land. Even whilst walking through the streets in company with another, he was not idle; for if his companion bowed to a white person he would rebuke him, and observe that all men were born equal, and that he was surprised that anyone would degrade himself by such conduct, that he would never cringe to the whites, nor ought anyone who had the feelings of a man. When answered, "We are slaves," he would sarcastically and indignantly reply, "You deserve to remain slaves"; and if he were further asked, "What can we do," he would remark, "Go and buy a spelling book and read the fable of Hercules and the Waggoner"; which he would then repeat, and apply it to their situation. He also sought every opportunity of entering into conversation with white persons when they could be overheard by Negroes near by, especially in grogshops, during which conversation he would artfully introduce some bold remark on slavery; and sometimes, when from the character he was conversing with he found he might be still bolder, he would go so far, that had not his declarations in such situations been clearly proved, they would scarcely have been credited. He continued this course until sometime after the commencement of the last winter; by which time he had not only obtained incredible influence among persons of color, but many feared him more than their owners, and one of them declared, even more than his God.

At this period he sounded Rolla and Ned, two slaves of his Excellency Thomas Bennett, and finding them ready to acquiesce in his schemes, he made the same proposals to Jack, belonging to

Mrs. Purcell, and Peter, belonging to Mr. Poyas, who also consented with equal promptness. These men were his first four associates, three of whom, viz. Rolla, Ned, and Peter, immediately became his most active agents. Sometime after Christmas he was also joined by Gullah Jack, belonging to Mr. Pritchard, and subsequently by Monday, belonging to Mr. Gell; who soon proved themselves to be as fit men for his purpose, and as active as Rolla, Ned, and Peter. These constituted his five principal officers, by whose means, aided by some others whom he employed to go and travel about the country adjacent to Charleston, and among the latter, the principal agents being Lot Forrester and Frank Ferguson, he engaged great numbers to join in the intended insurrection. He also at his house held nocturnal meetings for the purpose of interchanging opinions, maturing the plan, and collecting and giving information, at which meetings numbers of the insurgents, both from country and town attended, and where collections were made for the purpose of providing arms and ammunition, and for defraying such expences as might be indispensably necessary. He also attended meetings at other places appointed by himself, at one place in particular on Charleston Neck, about two miles and a half from the city. Besides his five principal officers already mentioned, he had other recruiting agents, though on a smaller scale, among whom were William Palmer, William Garner, Charles Drayton, and Peirault Strohecker. In order to induce the colored population to join them, every principle which could operate upon the mind of man was artfully employed: religion, hope, fear, and deception, were resorted to as occasion required. All were told, and many believed, that God approved of their designs; those whose fears would have restrained them, were forced to yield by threats of death; those whose prudence and foresight induced them to pause, were cheered with the assurance that assistance from Santo Domingo and Africa were at hand; whilst those upon whom none of these principles operated, were excited from despair on being informed, that the whites, perceiving they were becoming too numerous, had resolved to create a false alarm of fire, and as they came out in the dead of night to kill them, in order to thin their numbers. And strange as it may appear, yet vast numbers of the Africans firmly believed that Gullah Jack was a sorcerer; that he

could neither be killed nor taken; and that whilst they retained
the charms which he had distributed they would themselves be
invulnerable. Add to all this, their belief that Congress had eman-
cipated them, and we may readily credit the declaration of Monday Gell and Peirault, that they never spoke to any person of
color on the subject, or knew of anyone who had been spoken
to by the other leaders, who had withheld his assent. Vesey being
a free man encountered none of those obstacles which would have
been in the way of a slave; his time was at his own disposal, and
he could go wherever he pleased, without interruption, qualifica-
tions and advantages absolutely necessary for the Chief in a
Conspiracy, and which enabled him to travel so much about the
country as he did.

On perusing the testimony, the declaration of one or two of
the witnesses that this plot had been in agitation for four years
will strike the observation of everyone; but it must not be supposed therefrom, that recruiting or enlisting had been progressing
for that time; or that, for that time there existed any direct proposal from Vesey or anyone else for such a measure. Such was
not the case. No active measures were taken until near last
Christmas. In speaking of this attempt being in agitation for four
years, allusion was had to Vesey's conduct and language during
that time, and to the dissatisfaction which appeared since to exist
amongst the colored population. This was about the time that the
African congregation (so-called from its being composed wholly
of persons of color and almost entirely of blacks) was formed,
and their Church built in Hampstead;[5] of which Vesey had been
a member, and of which his principal associates, Gullah Jack,
Monday, Ned, and Peter, were also members; and the two last,
were class leaders. It was also about this time, that class meetings
of the colored people had become so common as they now are;
each class having a colored preacher or leader as they were
termed, named by the Minister of the Church to which he belonged; at which meetings, held usually at night in some retired
building, avowedly for religious instruction and worship, no white
person attended. That inflammatory and insurrectionary doctrines,
without any direct proposal for such an attempt, were inculcated
at these meetings or some of them, was positively proved; and

further, that they were to be used as places of rendezvous and rallying points for communicating to all, the exact night and hour, on which the first blow was to be struck. The great impropriety of allowing meetings of any kind to be held solely by slaves, and at such times and places, must forcibly strike every reflecting mind. The African congregation above mentioned was not only composed altogether of colored persons, but their Ministers were also colored; and were stated to have been regularly ordained Bishops and Ministers of the Gospel. The influence which such men and class leaders must necessarily acquire over the minds of the ignorant blacks is evident; and if a disposition exists in them to obtain for their own color and themselves, the freedom and privileges enjoyed by the whites, by enlisting into their cause perverted religion and fanaticism, that desperation is kindled in their hearers, the consequences of which are but too well known. Is it to be wondered at that, under all the foregoing circumstances, an attempt to create an insurrection should be contemplated!

Vesey, perceiving that so far everything had answered his most sanguine expectations, himself in possession of vast influence over his own color, and their minds poisoned and embittered against the white population, began about Christmas 1821, to probe those whom he had selected as leaders; and found as he expected a ready acquiescence in his measures by all of them except Monday Gell, who wavered for some time before he joined. In the selection of his leaders, Vesey showed great penetration and sound judgment. Rolla was plausible, and possessed uncommon self-possession; bold and ardent, he was not to be deterred from his purpose by danger. Ned's appearance indicated that he was a man of firm nerves, and desperate courage. Peter was intrepid and resolute, true to his engagements, and cautious in observing secrecy where it was necessary; he was not to be daunted nor impeded by difficulties, and though confident of success, was careful in providing against any obstacles or casualties which might arise, and intent upon discovering every means which might be in their power if thought of before hand. Gullah Jack was regarded as a sorcerer, and as such feared by the natives of Africa, who believe in witchcraft. He was not only considered invulnerable, but that he could make others so by his charms; and that he could and certainly would provide all his followers with arms. He was artful, cruel, bloody; his disposition in short was diabolical. His influence among the Africans was inconceivable. Monday was firm, resolute, discreet, and intelligent.

With these men as his principal officers, among whom Peter and Monday were certainly the most active, Vesey began to seduce others at the commencement of the present year. Peter and Monday (and probably the other leaders) kept lists of those who had joined their company or band. As Monday did not join until the business of enlisting had considerably progressed, and proceeded very prudently himself, he had but few on his list, according to his own confession only forty-two; but Peter who had consented as soon as spoken to, and was bold and active in his exertions, had six hundred names on his list, whom he had engaged in Charleston, from that division of the city in which he resided, which was South Bay. Peter also had in his possession another list of names, or as the witness afterwards explained himself, a memorandum of the whole number engaged, and who amounted as the witness was told to nine thousand, partly from the country and partly from the city. It is true that the witness who made these assertions did not see the lists himself, but he heard it from one who was in daily communication with Peter, and who was then endeavoring, and succeeded in inducing the witness to join; and as Peter wrote a good hand and was active throughout the whole affair, it is impossible to doubt but that he had such lists; but whether the numbers mentioned were really engaged or not, there is no mode of ascertaining, and it is more than probable that they were greatly exaggerated, and perhaps designedly so. That Peter was engaged in enlisting, was positively proved, but so scrupulously and resolutely to the last did he observe his pledge of secrecy to his associates, *that of the whole number arrested and tried, not one of them belonged to Peter's company.* Monday acknowledged that he kept a list, but only because he became state's evidence does that seem true. In the course of the trials it was also stated that Vesey had a variety of papers and books relating to this transaction, *which he burned when the discovery of the intended attempt was made.* Monday also burned his list, *and probably so did Peter at the same time.*

As these leaders only communicated to each other the numbers, and not the names of those whom they had engaged, and who constituted their company, and as with the exception of Monday, none of them betrayed their associates; the companies of Vesey, Peter, Ned, Rolla, and Gullah Jack have escaped detection and punishment; with the exception of a few of Gullah Jack's band, who were discovered in consequence of one of his men betraying those companions he knew, together with his leader.

In enlisting men the great caution observed by the leaders was remarkable. Few if any domestic servants were spoken to, as they were distrusted, and all who were consulted were told, that death would certainly await them if they informed; and Peter while he urged one of his agents to speak to others and solicit them to join, at the same time gave him this charge, "But take care and don't mention it to those waiting men who receive presents of old coats from their masters, or they'll betray us; *I* will speak to them." The enlistments appear to have been principally confined to Negroes hired or working out, such as carters, draymen, sawyers, porters, laborers, stevedores, mechanics, those employed in lumber yards, and in short to those who had certain allotted hours at their own disposal, and to the neighboring country Negroes. When the proposal was made to anyone to join, such arguments or threats were made use of as would ensure success, and which the leaders had been cautious to prepare beforehand, and suit to the different tempers and dispositions they would have to deal with.

As Vesey, from whom all orders emanated, and perhaps to whom only all important information was conveyed, died without confessing anything, any opinion formed as to the numbers actually engaged in the plot, must be altogether conjectural; but enough has been disclosed to satisfy every reasonable mind, that considerable numbers were concerned. Indeed the plan of attack, which embraced so many points to be assailed at the same instant, affords sufficient evidence of the fact.

The extent of country around Charleston which was embraced in this attempt, has not been so precisely ascertained as to be traced on a map with as much certainty as a division line between two states; but enough has been discovered, to induce a belief, that it extended to the north of Charleston many miles towards Santee, and unquestionably into St. John's Parish, to the south to James' and John's Islands, and to the west beyond Bacon's Bridge over Ashley River. That all who inhabited this extent of country were engaged in the plot, will not be pretended; it was not necessary or perhaps advisable, for at the season of the year in which the attempt was to be made, all the planters and their families are compelled to be absent from their plantations. If therefore a small number on a plantation or in the neighborhood were engaged in the plot, and acquainted with the precise night and hour of its execution, it would be an easy matter for them in the course of the preceding day, or within a few hours of their taking their own departure, to induce many others whose minds were already poisoned to proceed with them. In St. John's Parish four entire plantations of Negroes were engaged by Frank Ferguson, as he declared to one of the witnesses; and his statement receives great strength, from the letter of his owner to one of the authors, in reply to one from him requesting certain information in writing:

CONCLUSION OF THOMAS PARKER'S LETTER
OF 15TH SEPTEMBER, 1822, ADDRESSED
TO JAMES FERGUSON, ESQ.

If in this statement I am incorrect, do furnish me with a full one of what it was you did, especially as to what passed between the Governor and yourself, in relation to the Negroes in St. John's.

JAMES FERGUSON'S REPLY

Charleston, 16th *September,* 1822.

TO THOMAS PARKER, *Esq.*

Sir—As I perceive by your letter of yesterday, that your memory is not altogether correct with regard to my going up to my plantation on the business connected with the late attempt at insurrection, I shall endeavor to comply with your request, by relating transactions as they occurred.

About 26th or 27th June, Mr. Wesner, one of the committee of vigilance, had the politeness to communicate to me, that he had received information that my servants Frank and Adam, were concerned in the insurrection; and asked me whether I had a fellow named John, and one named Pompey in the country! He then took me to the Work House to examine Jesse Blackwood [then under sentence of death,] from whom the information was received; immediately upon leaving the room I told Mr. Wesner I was satisfied of the truth of Jesse's evidence. I directly brought Frank and Adam before the Court; you recollect that Frank was used as state's evidence and Adam discharged.

Jesse's evidence, as regards the country Negroes, was that he was to have gone to summon them down, that on his arrival he was to have asked for John and Pompey, that John was called John O—— and that one was a cooper; and that he was not to be seen by the driver: these directions were given him by Frank. Upon examining Frank a day or two after, he confirmed what Jesse had said; and said that John and Pompey and several others had agreed to come to town in case the insurrection began, or as he expressed it, "in case such things took place."

Thinking it my duty to inform the proper public authorities of my knowledge of the insurgents, and being anxious that if my Negroes were to be tried, they should have the benefit of such a Court as was then organized; on Friday, 28th June, I waited on the Governor and informed him that the insurrection had extended to my plantation, that two fellows were particularly named, and that if he thought proper to have them apprehended, I would assist personally any officers he might choose to send. He said it would be a great pity those poor wretches should suffer upon slight evidence; I then stated to him the evidence of Jesse and Frank; he said there was a Court organized which with the committees appointed appeared to take the entire management of the business. He expressed some regret at a misunderstanding with the Court, by which he had been at first prevented, having such communication with some of the criminals as he could have wished. After this short conversation, I said explicitly to him, then, sir, you do not intend to apprehend those Negroes. He replied he would not like to take upon himself the responsibility. From the Governor's house I went immediately to the Court Room, and formally gave to the Court and intendant the same information I had given to the Governor, they declined their interference only upon the ground that my plantation was beyond their jurisdiction.

On Saturday, 29th June, I went into the country and had John and Pompey severely corrected in the presence of the other Negro men on the plantation; but neither from them, nor from the others could I get any confession that they were at all cognizant of the intended plot. I gave orders to my driver to press on them the inutility of denying what was so fully proved against them; and to inform me of any confession they might make. I returned to town the next day, and for the four succeeding weeks, to my great astonishment I could get no acknowledgment through the messenger who came to me weekly. I then sent up a confidential old Negro who returned and told me, that the Negroes were ready to confess all to me, and had been so for some time past, but were prevented by the driver who was as much concerned as any of them. The next day [30th July,] I went into the country and sent the driver to town to be committed to the Work House, where he is now in confinement.

The confession of the Negroes went to say, that when Frank drove me from Georgetown to the plantation, which was about 10th June, he told them Denmark Vesey's stories, and said they must come to town and assist. And although they would not acknowledge that they had actually consented to come, yet I am of opinion, that they were so thoroughly convinced that the Negroes would succeed in their attempt, that they did intend to obey the summons of any messenger that should have reached them.

From the time I first heard that Frank had spoken of the

intended insurrection, at my plantation, and from my knowledge of the means ordinarily used by Negroes in communicating intelligence from one plantation to another; I was of
opinion that it was well known through the neighborhood,
and my visit of two days on 30, and 31st July, gave me an
opportunity of being confirmed in my opinion—and if it would
not exceed the limits of a letter, I would willingly detail the
minutiæ by which I was so confirmed.

By the confession of some of my most intelligent Negroes,
it appears that reports of their emancipation had of late
years been much in circulation; but they said, that until
Frank told them, they had no idea it was to be effected in
the manner proposed by Denmark Vesey. In various conversations with Frank he always persisted in saying he had no
knowledge of Denmark Vesey's plot until 1st May, 1822;
which assertion I could not reconcile with several conversations of his on freedom, which I had traced back to nine
months before that time; but he explained it by stating that
Billy Palmer was the first who told him of the rights of the
blacks, two summers ago.

The orderly conduct of the Negroes in any district of
country within 40 miles of Charleston, is no evidence that
they were ignorant of the intended attempt. A more orderly
gang than my own is not to be found in this state—and one
of Denmark Vesey's directions was, that they should assume
the most implicit obedience.

Very respectfully, I have the honor to be, your most
obedient servant.

JAMES FERGUSON.

Thomas Parker, Esq.

It was principally for the attempt of Jesse (one of the conspirators), to go to Mr. Ferguson's plantation in St. John's, to inform the Negroes of the night and hour they were to be in Charleston, that he was executed; though the declarations made by him
independently of this act, showed that he had heartily embarked
in the plot. It was in testimony that the Insurgents "were trying all round the country, from Georgetown and Santee, round

about to Combahec to get people," and subsequent to the determination of the trials, it has been distinctly ascertained, that Vesey had been in the country as far north as South Santee; and southwardly from Charleston as fas as the Euhaws; which is between seventy and eighty miles from the city.

During the period that these enlistments were carrying on, Vesey held frequent meetings of the conspirators at his house; and as arms were necessary to their success, each night, a hat was handed round, and collections made, for the purpose of purchasing them, and also to defray other necessary expenses. A Negro, who was a blacksmith and had been accustomed to make edged tools, was employed to make pike heads and bayonets with sockets, to be fixed at the ends of long poles and used as pikes. Of these pike heads and bayonets, one hundred were said to have been made at an early day, and by the 16th June, as many as two or three hundred, and between three and four hundred daggers. At one time, Gullah Jack was seen by several witnesses with six of the pike heads, which he said he had just brought from the blacksmith's; and a bundle containing upwards of twelve well selected poles, neatly trimmed and smoothed off, and about nine or ten feet long, were found concealed on the farm on Charleston Neck, where several of their meetings were held; and which were carried there to have the pike heads and bayonets fixed on them. These were brought before the Court: how many more may have been carried there, and were afterwards removed, destroyed, or effectually concealed, or how many more would have been carried there had the plot not been discovered, is altogether a matter of conjecture; but certain it is, that twelve or twenty poles were more than were requisite for only six pike heads, and as those six pike heads have not been found, there is no reason for disbelieving the testimony of there having been many more made. To presume that the insurgents had no arms because none were seized, would be drawing an inference in direct opposition to the whole of the evidence. Besides the arms above-mentioned, it was proved that Peter had a sword; that Charles Drayton had a gun and sword; that John Horry had a sword; that Pharo Thompson had a scythe converted into a sword; that Adam Yates had a knife, such as are used by riflemen as dirks, but which from its length was more properly a sword; that Monday had a sword; that Bacchus Hammet gave Peirault a sword and carried another and a pistol to Vesey, together with a keg of powder, that was afterwards made up into fixed ammunition, and which he had stolen from his owner; and that some of the arms of the Revenue Cutter had been stolen, yet none of these arms were found. A dagger rudely made, was found in Rolla's trunk; a quantity of slow match which was supposed to have been stolen out of the Arensal by Lot was found concealed on one of the wharves, with which the city was to have been fired; and a very considerable number of musket balls were accidentally discovered, concealed under water in one of the docks. But the means which the insurgents had in their power of arming themselves were ample. On King Street, beyond the limits of the city considerably, though within the lines, in a common wooden store, unguarded, were deposited the arms of the Neck Company of Militia, amounting to between two and three hundred muskets and bayonets, and a few swords; the door of which store was to have been opened by Bacchus Hammet immediately as the insurgents appeared before it, which a party were to have done at the appointed hour. At Mr. Duqereron's store on King Street, also beyond the limits of the city, and but a short distance below the last mentioned store, were deposited for sale about five hundred muskets and bayonets; to which store a body of the same party were to have gone at the appointed hour and secured those arms. To assist in effecting their several purposes, Vesey had made a collection purposely to purchase dark lanterns. Mr. Schirer's store in Queen Street, and the other stores with arms, were noted by the chiefs as magazines of arms to which they could resort; especially the stores of those gunsmiths, with whom the arms of some of the militia companies are deposited for the purpose of being kept in order. But in addition to these means, the Arsenal in Meeting Street opposite St. Michael's Church, in which the greatest proportion of the arms of the State are deposited, was to have been forced and the arms seized. Let it be remembered that this Arsenal is on the public street, without even a brick wall in front of it, with doors not stronger than those of many dwelling houses, and the difficulty of forcing it will not appear very great. The slaves who were enlisted in Charleston were to endeavor to purloin their owner's arms, and there appeared to be a confidence in the leaders, that a sufficient number in Charleston would from different sources be provided with arms to enable them in the first moments of surprise, and before the whites could possibly assemble, completely to succeed in their first attacks on the Guard House, and the unguarded Arsenals and stores containing arms; after which they would be at no loss for arms. The Negroes from the country were also to bring with them their hoes, hatchets, axes, and spades, which might either be used as offensive weapons, or as instruments to break open doors. Had the plot not been discovered, and the insurrection commenced at the appointed time, they would not have been found unarmed.

Vesey had originally fixed upon the night of the second Monday in July for the attack, as about that time the number of the white inhabitants in the city would be much diminished; those who are either going to the North, or to Sullivan's Island, or into the upper parts of the State to spend the summer, generally depart before that time; a circumstance which had not escaped the observation of Vesey. However, in consequence of the discoveries made on the 30th May, and the apprehension of Peter and Mingo Harth the day after (but who after being examined were discharged), Vesey thought it prudent to fix upon an earlier day for the attack, and changed it sometime after to the night of Sunday the 16th of June. Though he was able to communicate this change to his associates in the city, it would appear from his sending messengers into the country as late as the very day preceding the night on which the attempt was to be made, that he had not had sufficient time, or found some difficulty in communicating to his followers in the country; which accounts for their not generally appearing in the city on the night of the 16th of June. Twenty or thirty men however in a canoe did reach the city, and immediately had their arrival reported to Vesey; and with this in view many of those who came into the city on Saturday night and during Sunday may have visited Charleston, on which day, great numbers (certainly above a thousand as will presently be shown) invariably repair to the city; but the preparations made by the whites, and the number of troops on duty that night, convinced him and his followers that their plot was discovered and the whites on their guard; and as their hope of success was founded on effecting a surprise, Vesey sent them word to depart from the city as soon as possible and wait for further orders; "and the conspirators finding the whole town encompassed at ten o'clock by the most vigilant patrols, did not dare to show themselves, whatever might have been their plans. In the progress of the investigation, it was distinctly in proof, that but for those military demonstrations, the effort would unquestionably have been made; and that a meeting took place on Sunday afternoon, the 16th at four o'clock, of several of the ringleaders at Denmark Vesey's, for the purpose of making their preliminary arrangements."

The plan of attack as originally formed was still adhered to, with the exception of the change of time before mentioned. It was to commence precisely at twelve o'clock on the night of Sunday the 16th of June; at which hour everyone was to move, and the attack at every point to be made at the same moment. Peter was to lead a party which was to assemble on South Bay, and to be joined by a force from James' Island; he was then to march up and seize the Arsenal and Guard House opposite St. Michael's Church and secure the arms. From this force, a party was to be detached, whose duty it would be to prevent the citizens from assembling at their alarm posts, by cutting them off as they arrived. A second body consisting partly of Negroes from the country and from the Neck, was to assemble on the Neck, under the command of Ned, and to seize the Arsenal there. A third to assemble at Bennett's Mills, to be headed by Rolla, and, after murdering the Governor and Intendant, to march through the city, or take his station at Cannon's Bridge, and thus prevent the inhabitants of Cannonsborough from entering the city. A fourth, partly from the country, and partly from that portion of the city, was to rendezvous on Gadsden's Wharf, march and attack the upper Guard House. A fifth, of country and Neck Negroes, for whom in particular the pikes which were made had been provided, was to assemble at Bulkley's farm, about two miles and a half from the city, and seize the powder magazine three miles and a half from town, and then march into the city; and a sixth to

assemble at Vesey's, and under his command, to march down to
the Guard House. While these attacks were going on, a number
of them on horseback were to ride through the streets and kill
every person they might meet, and prevent them from assembling,
or extending the alarm. Batteau was to join and march down
with Vesey; and Gullah Jack with another body, which was to
assemble in Boundary Street at the head of King Street, was to
take possession of the arms of the Neck Company, which were
deposited in a store as before-mentioned, and also those in Mr.
Duquercron's store. Arms thus being provided from these different
sources, the city was to have been fired, and an indiscriminate
slaughter of the whites to commence, and also those of their own
color who had not joined them, or did not immediately do so. It
was determined that no one should be neuter; "he that is not with
me is against me" [6] was their creed. The leaders appeared to have
no doubt but that those slaves who had not been particularly
spoken to would join them, as soon as the insurrection had fairly
commenced, and the most partial success had been attained. "Let
us assemble a sufficient number to commence the work with spirit
and we'll not want men, they'll fall in behind us fast enough."

Among those unacquainted with the employments, habits, and
customs of the inhabitants of Charleston and the country and
Islands immediately surrounding it, a doubt might arise, how the
insurgents were to provide themselves with horses in the city;
and how the Negroes from the Islands and the opposite sides of
Ashley and Cooper rivers would find a conveyance to town. In
neither of these respects, however, was there the least difficulty.
There were four sources from which they intended to obtain
horses; the three first not only feasible but certain, the last more
difficult, but by no means insurmountable. First, numbers of the
draymen and carters of the city, who are all persons of color,
and many of whom have their horses both day and night under
their control, (those who are free keeping them in their own yards,
and many of the slaves keeping their horses out of their owner's)
were to act as horsemen; so were, secondly, some of the butcher's
boys, who could with ease provide themselves with horses; thirdly,
the slaves at some of the public livery stables were engaged in
the plot, and were a short time before the appointed hour to have

the horses saddled, and at the hour to open the stable doors, and thus provide their comrades with horses; and fourthly, some of those whose owners were attached to either of the corps of cavalry in the city, were to endeavor to seize and bring off with them their owner's horses. As to the means which those on the Islands would have to reach Charleston, they were abundant. The immense number of canoes of various sizes (many of which could transport upwards of one hundred men), employed in bringing to the Charleston market, vegetables, stock of every kind, and the staple of the country, would have afforded conveyance for thousands. As a matter of information and precaution, the Intendant of Charleston during the trials and investigations of the plot, when Negroes were rather fearful of coming into town, directed numbers of those who came over in such boats on Sundays from the Islands to be counted, when even at that time, upwards of five hundred entered the city on one Sunday. From this statement some estimate may be formed of the number of Negroes who ordinarily come into Charleston on Sunday from different parts of the country; of the facility of transportation afforded by these canoes to those on the islands and rivers, and the foresight of Vesey in fixing on Sunday night for the attack, as on that day the slaves might leave their owner's plantations and come into town without being particularly noticed, which would on any other day be just the reverse.

The attention of the leaders to the most minute particulars is worthy of observation. In order to ensure the assemblage of the insurgents at the exact moment, the Negroes who lived near the places of meeting, were requested for that night to conceal in their owner's premises one or more of their comrades; at least Gullah Jack was pursuing this plan, and as it was proved that the order emanated from Vesey, the same orders were no doubt extended to the others. A white man in this city who was a barber and hair dresser, was employed to make a number of wigs and false whiskers of the hair of white persons for some of the insurgents, with the assistance of these, and by painting their faces, they hoped in the darkness of the night and in the confusion to be mistaken for white men. Such a plan as this would no doubt have assisted Peter in his bold determination to advance singly some distance ahead of his party, and surprise and put to death the sentinel before the Guard House. These wigs and whiskers were the only means by which Vesey was thrown off his guard during his imprisonment. The hair dresser who had been employed was carried by the Intendant into Vesey's cell, and Vesey was asked if he knew that man. With the greatest effrontery and composure he denied having ever seen him; at which moment, the Intendant took out of his pocket the very wig made for Vesey himself, which had such an effect upon him, that he exclaimed "Good God"—remained silent a moment or two, and then acknowledged that the wig was made for him and that he knew the man.

The principal features in the plan of attack above-given were proved by most of the witnesses; but some of them omitted parts, and some stated other particulars, which it would perhaps be tedious and unnecessary to mention. In addition to the foregoing circumstances, it was proved and subsequently acknowledged by Monday, that Vesey had written two letters to Santo Domingo on the subject of this plot;[7] but of the character, extent, and importance of the correspondence, no satisfactory information has been obtained, and perhaps by no other person but Vesey could this have been given.

What were the views and plans of the insurgents after they had taken Charleston, had they succeeded in doing so, does not satisfactorily appear, and it is probable they had formed none, but intended to regulate themselves according to circumstances; but they appeared confident, that they would have been joined by such numbers from the country, as to have been able, at that particular season of the year, and with the fortifications on the Neck and around the Harbor, to have retained possession of the city, as long as they might deem it expedient. One or two of the insurgents said, that Vesey, after robbing the banks of specie, and plundering the city of all that was most valuable, intended to sail for Santo Domingo with his principal adherents; but the informants themselves spoke of it more as a suggestion, than a fixed plan.

The character and condition of most of the insurgents were

such, as rendered them objects the least liable to suspicion. It is a melancholy truth, that the general good conduct of all the leaders, except Gullah Jack, had secured to them not only the unlimited confidence of their owners, but they had been indulged in every comfort, and allowed every privilege compatible with their situation in the community; and although Gullah Jack was not remarkable for the correctness of his deportment, he by no means sustained a bad character. Vesey himself was free, and had amassed a considerable estate for one of his color; he was in good business as a carpenter, and enjoyed so much the confidence of the whites, that when he was accused, the charge was not only discredited, but he was not even arrested for several days after, and not until the proof of his guilt had become too strong to be doubted.[8] It is difficult to conceive what motive he had to enter into such a plot, unless it was the one mentioned by one of the witnesses, who said that Vesey had several children who were slaves, and that he said on one occasion he wished to see them free, as he himself artfully remarked in his defence on his trial; yet with him it unquestionably originated, and by him was headed. Rolla was the confidential servant of his master; so much so, that when his master's public duties required his absence from his family, they were left under the protection of that slave; and yet that very man, undertook to head a party, whose first act was to be the murder of that master, who had reposed such confidence in him, and had treated him with great kindness. Ned was also a confidential servant, and his general good conduct was commendable. Peter was a slave of great value, and for his color, a first rate ship carpenter. He possessed the confidence of his master, in a remarkable degree, and had been treated with indulgence, liberality, and kindness. Monday enjoyed all the substantial comforts of a free man; (he was) much indulged and trusted by his master; his time and a large porportion of the profits of his labor were at his own disposal. He even kept his master's *arms* and sometimes his money. He is a most excellent harnessmaker, and kept his shop in Meeting Street. Monday is an *Ebo*, and is now in the prime of life, having been in the country fifteen or twenty years. But not only were the leaders of good character and much indulged by their owners, but this was very generally the case with all who were convicted, many of them possessing the highest confidence of their owners, *and not one of bad character.*

Another characteristic of this plot was, that a decided majority of the insurgents, either did or had belonged to the African Congregation, among whom the enlistments were principally and successfully carried on. From the testimony, the presumptions of innocence are in favor of the Bishops and Ministers (as they styled themselves) of the Congregation; but two of them have left the state under strong suspicions of having favored the plot. The class leaders appointed by them, certainly did belong; two of whom were principals, and Vesey their chief and a fourth leader though not class leaders, yet belonged to the Congregation, Rolla being the only exception.

The conduct and behavior of Vesey and his five leaders during their trial and imprisonment, may be interesting to many. When Vesey was tried, he folded his arms and seemed to pay great attention to the testimony given against him, but with his eyes fixed on the floor. In this situation he remained immovable, until the witnesses had been examined by the Court and cross-examined by his counsel; when he requested permission to examine the witnesses himself. He at first questioned them in the dictatorial, despotic manner, in which he was probably accustomed to address them; but this not producing the desired effect, he questioned them with affected surprise and concern for bearing false testimony against him; still failing in his purpose, he then examined them strictly as to dates, but could not make them contradict themselves. The evidence being closed, he addressed the Court at considerable length, in which his principal endeavor was to impress them with the idea, that as his situation in life had been such that he could have had no inducement to join in such an attempt, the charge against him must be false; and he attributed it to the great hatred which he alleged the blacks had against him; but his allegations were unsupported by proof. When he received his sentence, the tears trickled down his cheeks; and it is not improbable if he had been placed in a separate cell, he might have made important discoveries; but confined as four of the convicts were in one room, they "mutually supported each other; and died obedient to the

stern and emphatic injunction of their comrade, Peter Poyas":
"Do not open your lips! Die silent, as you shall see me do." Rolla
when arraigned, affected not to understand the charge against
him, and when it was at his request further explained to him, assumed with wonderful adroitness, astonishment, and surprise. He
was remarkable throughout his trial, for great presence and composure of mind. When he was informed he was convicted and was
advised to prepare for death, though he had previously (but after
his trial), confessed his guilt, he appeared perfectly confounded,
but exhibited no signs of fear. In Ned's behavior there was nothing
remarkable, but his countenance was stern and immovable, even
while he was receiving the sentence of death; from his looks it
was impossible to discover or conjecture what were his feelings.
Not so with Peter, for in his countenance were strongly marked
disappointed ambition, revenge, indignation, and an anxiety to
know how far the discoveries had extended, and the same emotions
were exhibited in his conduct. He did not appear to fear personal
consequences, for his whole behavior indicated the reverse; but
exhibited an evident anxiety for the success of their plan, in which
his whole soul was embarked. His countenance and behavior were
the same when he received his sentence, and his only words were
on retiring, "I suppose you'll let me see my wife and family before
I die?" and that not in a supplicating tone. When he was asked a
day or two after, if it was possible he could wish to see his master
and family murdered who had treated him so kindly, he only replied to the question by a smile. Monday's behavior was not peculiar. When he was before the Court his arms were folded; he
heard the testimony given against him, and received his sentence
with the utmost firmness and composure. "But no description can
accurately convey to others, the impression which the trial, defence
and appearance of Gullah Jack made on those who witnessed the
workings of his cunning and rude address." When arrested and
brought before the Court in company with another African named
Jack, the property of the estate of Pritchard, he assumed so much
ignorance, and looked and acted the fool so well, that some of the
Court could not believe that this was the Necromancer who was
sought after. This conduct he continued when on his trial, until
he saw the witnesses and heard the testimony as it progressed

against him; when in an instant, his countenance was lighted up as if by lightning, and "his wildness and vehemence of gesture, and the malignant glance with which he eyed the witnesses who appeared against him, all indicated the savage, who indeed had been caught but not tamed." His courage, however, soon forsook him. When he received sentence of death, he earnestly implored that a fortnight longer might be allowed him, and then that a week longer, which he continued earnestly to solicit until he was taken from the Court Room to his cell; and when he was carried to execution "he gave up his spirit without firmness or composure." He was sentenced on the 9th July to be hanged on the 12th.

The whole number arrested were one hundred and thirty-one, of whom sixty-seven were convicted. From among those convicted, thirty-five were executed; the remainder will be sent beyond the limits of the United States, as well as some of those who though not convicted, are morally guilty; and of those who suffered death, twenty-two were executed at the same time, on the same gallows. The object of punishment being effectually attained by these examples, and the ringleaders being convicted, the arrests stopped here.

One who was not a member of the Court, cannot well conceive the effect produced by the threats used, in preventing a discovery of the plot. The enlistments had been going on and the preparations making actively since Christmas, yet it was not until the 30th May, that the least suspicion was entertained by the whites. Had it not been that one, not authorized by Vesey or the other leaders and evidently unfit for such a purpose, undertook to enlist, no discovery might have been made; for though the information received on the 14th June was infinitely more extensive and in detail, and from a very different quarter, yet the first communication and the excitement it occasioned, might have had considerable effect in eliciting the other. The information received on the 30th May, however, so far from leading to a discovery of the plot, was eventually disbelieved; so that the detection was not really made, until two nights preceding the intended exhibition of the dreadful tragedy. The discovery of the plot, however, in sufficient time, in this, as in every other instance, enabled the constituted authorities to crush it in the bud.

The information received on the 30th of May, was communicated to the Intendant of Charleston about three o'clock in the afternoon, by a gentleman of great respectability, who that morning had returned from the country. This gentleman stated, "That a favorite and confidential slave of his had communicated to him, on his arrival in town, a conversation which had taken place at the market on the Saturday preceding, between himself and a black man, which afforded strong reasons for believing that a revolt and insurrection were in contemplation among a proportion at least of our black population. The corporation was forthwith summoned to meet at five o'clock, for the purpose of hearing the narrative of the slave who had given this information to his master, to which meeting the attendance of His Excellency the Governor was solicited; with which invitation he promptly complied. Between however, the hours of three and five o'clock, the gentleman who had conveyed the information to the Intendant, having again examined his slave, was induced to believe, that the Negro fellow who had communicated the intelligence of the intended revolt to the slave in question, belonged to Messrs. J. & D. Paul, Broad Street, and resided in their premises. Accordingly, with a promptitude worthy of all praise, without waiting for the interposition of the civil authority he applied to the Messrs. Paul, and had the whole of their male servants committed to the Guard House, until the individual who had accosted the slave of this gentleman, on the occasion previously mentioned, could be identified from among them.

On the assembling of the corporation at five, the slave of this gentleman was brought before them, having previously identified Mr. Paul's William as the man who had accosted him in the market, he then related the following circumstances:

"On Saturday afternoon last (my master being out of town) I went to market; after finishing my business I strolled down the wharf below the fish-market, from which I observed a small vessel in the stream with a singular flag; whilst looking at this object, a black man (Mr. Paul's William), came up to me and remarking the subject which engaged my attention said, I have often seen a flag with the number 76 on it, but never with 96, before. After some trifling conversation on this point, he remarked with considerable earnestness to me. Do you know that something serious is about to take place? To which I replied no. Well, said he, there is, and many of us are determined to right ourselves! I asked him to explain himself—when he remarked, why, we are determined to shake off our bondage, and for this purpose we stand on a good foundation, many have joined, and if you will go with me, I will show you the man, who has the list of names who will take yours down. I was so much astonished and horror struck at this information, that it was a moment or two before I could collect myself sufficient to tell him I would have nothing to do with this business, that I was satisfied with my condition, that I was grateful to my master for his kindness and wished no change. I left him instantly, lest, if this fellow afterwards got into trouble, and I had been seen conversing with him, in so public a place, I might be suspected and thrown into difficulty. I did not however remain easy under the burden of such a secret, and consequently determined to consult a free man of color named —— and to ask his advice. On conferring with this friend, he urged me with great earnestness to communicate what had passed between Mr. Paul's man and myself to my master, and not to lose a moment in so doing.[9] I took his advice and not waiting, even for the return of my master to town, I mentioned it to my mistress and young master. On the arrival of my master, he examined me as to what had passed, and I stated to him what I have mentioned to yourselves.

On this witness being dismissed from the presence of Council, the prisoner (William) was examined. The mode resorted to in his examination was to afford him no intimation of the subject of the information which had been lodged against him, as it was extremely desirable in the first place, to have the testimony of the other witness corroborated as to time and place, that, from the confessions of the prisoner himself, it might appear that he was at the fish-market at the period stated, and that a singular flag, flying on board of a schooner, had formed the subject of his observation. After a vast deal of equivocation, he admitted all these facts, but when the rest of his conversation was put home to him, he flatly denied it, but with so many obvious indications of guilt, that it was deemed unwise to discharge him. He was remanded for the night to the Guard House, it having been decided to subject him to solitary confinement in the black hole of the Work House, where, on the succeeding morning, he was to be conveyed.

On the morning of the 31st he was again examined by the attending warden at the Guard House (having during the night, made some disclosures to Captain Dove) on which occasion he admitted all the conversation which he had held at the fish-market, with the witness before mentioned, and stated that he had received his information from Mingo Harth, who was in possession of the muster roll of the insurgents.

With the hope of still further disclosures William was conveyed to the Work House and placed in solitary confinement. The individuals (Mingo Harth and Peter Poyas) against whom he gave information, as those who had communicated to him the intelligence of the plot for raising an insurrection, were forthwith taken up by the wardens, and their trunks examined. These fellows behaved with so much composure and coolness, and treated the charge alleged against them with so much levity—no writings being found in their chests, containing the smallest suspicion, excepting an enigmatical letter, which was then too obscure for explanation, and to which subsequent events only afforded a clue—that the wardens (Messrs. Wesner and Condy) were completely deceived and had these men discharged; but their movements were nevertheless watched, and measures of precaution taken. Things remained in this state for six or seven days, until about the 8th of June, when William, who had been a week in solitary confinement, beginning to fear that he would soon be led forth to the scaffold, for summary execution, confessed that he had for some time known of the plot, that it was very extensive, embracing an indiscriminate massacre of the whites, and that the blacks were to be headed by an individual, who carried about him a charm which rendered him invulnerable.

Three or four days now elapsed, and notwithstanding all our efforts, we could obtain no confirmation of the disclosures of William; on the contrary, they seemed to have sustained some invalidation from the circumstance of one of the individuals (Ned Bennett) whom he named as a person who had information in relation to the insurrection, coming voluntarily to the Intendant, and soliciting an examination, if he was an object of suspicion. In this stage of the business, it was not deemed advisable prematurely to press these examinations, as it might have a tendency to arrest any further developments.

On the night, however, of Friday the 14th, the information of William was amply confirmed, and details infinitely more abundant and interesting afforded. At eight o'clock on this evening, the Intendant received a visit from a gentleman, who is advantageously known in this community for his worth and respectability.

This gentleman, with an anxiety which the occasion was well calculated to beget, stated to the Intendant, that, having the most unbounded confidence in a faithful slave belonging to his family, who was distinguished alike for his uncommon intelligence and integrity, he was induced to inform him, that rumors were abroad of an intended insurrection of the blacks, and that it was said, that this movement had been traced to some of the colored members of Dr. Palmer's church, in which he was known to be a class leader. On being strongly enjoined to conceal nothing, he, the next day, Friday the 14th, came to his master, and informed him, that the fact was really so, that a public disturbance was contemplated by the blacks, and not a moment should be lost in informing the constituted authorities, as the succeeding Sunday, the 16th, at twelve o'clock at night, was the period fixed for the rising, which, if not prevented, would inevitably occur at that hour. This slave, it appears, was in no degree connected with the plot, but he had an intimate friend, A——— (one of his class) who had been trusted by the conspirators with the secret, and had been solicited by them to join their association; to this A——— first appeared to consent, but at no period absolutely sent in his adhesion. According to the statement which he afterwards made himself to the Court, it would seem that it was a subject of great regret and contrition with him, that he had ever appeared to lend his approbation to a scheme so wicked and atrocious, and that he sought occasion to make atonement, by divulging the plot, which on the 14th he did, to the slave of the gentleman in question, his class leader.[10]

As the account given by this slave was remarkably coincident with the one given by William, with whom he had had no communication, and also coincided in its most material points with the plan of attack just given, such measures were taken by his Excellency the Governor, as the occasion required. On the night appointed for the attack, the insurgents found a very strong guard on duty, and by ten o'clock the whole town was surrounded by the most vigilant patrols; they therefore dared not show themselves.

Notwithstanding the discovery which had been made, and the complete frustration of their plans, yet so true were they in observing their pledge of secrecy to each other, that of all those arrested up to the 22d June, only six of them were convicted. The discovery which had been made and the conviction of those six (among whom was their chief and three of his principal leaders, together with Batteau, who though not as principal a leader as the others was yet an officer), did not however induce them to lay aside their design. Subsequent to these arrests and convictions, it was proposed to make the attempt early on the morning of the 2d July, immediately after the nightly Guards and Patrols had been discharged from duty, and which would be at the beating of the Reveille; and some even had the boldness to propose a rescue and general attack, as the convicts were carried forth for execution. Their reason for fixing on so early a day was their anxiety to save their chief and leaders, who were on that day to be executed; but the time between the day on which those six were sentenced, and that on which they were to be executed, was too short, to enable them to concert proper measures; especially as the whites were now on the alert and watchful; and moreover, one of their two remaining leaders on whom they principally depended, was arrested the very day previous to the execution, a circumstance well calculated to disconcert and deter them. On the 5th July, further information was received from the slave of another gentleman, who voluntarily came forward and offered to reveal all the information he possessed, on condition that his name should never be disclosed. In addition to naming several of his associates, and describing the sorcerer Gullah Jack, who was his leader, so as to lead to his apprehension, he mentioned that the insurgents had by no means been induced to abandon their original design by the execution which had taken place on the second instant; and that their remaining leader Gullah Jack was actively extending the information, that he had resolved to rise and make the attack at day dawn on the morning of the 6th. Want of time to concert measures for this attack also, would probably have prevented its being made; but it was effectually stopped by the arrest of Gullah Jack on the day previous. On the 9th July, sentence of death was passed upon five more, two of whom were Monday and Gullah Jack, and a third, Charles, the slave of the Honorable John Drayton; who though not a leader, had taken so active a part in the business, as to be perhaps as much known in it as the leaders were. It was now thirty-nine days since the civil authorities had received information of this plot, and twenty during which the Court organized for the trial of the insurgents had been engaged (Sundays excepted); and yet, so true were they to each other, that during all that time only fifteen had been discovered whose connection in the plot was clear, of whom four were used as witnesses. After Monday Gell and Charles Drayton were convicted there appeared to be a pause in our further discoveries, and some prospect of the investigation closing with their execution and those of John Horry, Harry Haig, and Gullah Jack.

On the 9th of July, however, these five men, were called before the Court to receive sentence, and after it had been pronounced, with the most impressive solemnity, they were withdrawn to a common ward in the Work House for half an hour until separate cells could be provided for them. It was at this moment that Charles Drayton, overwhelmed with terror and guilt, went up to Monday and reproached him with having induced him to join in a scheme which had placed him in such a miserable and perilous situation. To this appeal Monday not only confessed his guilt, but observed to Charles that their present fate was justly and precisely what they had a right to expect, after their detected and defeated project. On which there immediately ensued between them a conversation on the extent of the guilt of others, in which Monday gave Charles the names of many accomplices whom he had not previously known in the plot; the arrival of the blacksmith to iron the convicts, and the turnkey to convey them to separate cells, interrupted the conversation.

Charles, during the night of the 9th, sent for Mr. Gordon, who has charge of the Work House, and informed him that he was extremely anxious to see the Intendant, as he had some important disclosures to make. By daylight, on the morning of the

10th, this message was conveyed to the person for whom it was intended, and Charles was visited at sunrise. He was found, in a state of the most lamentable depression and panic, and he seemed prepared to make the most ample declarations from the fear of death and the consequences of an *hereafter*, if he went out of the world without revealing all that he knew in relation to the conspiracy, in which he had been so active an agent. Before his narrative was received, he was most specially put on his guard, that no promises could be made to him of a reversal of his fate, but that he might rest satisfied, his condition could not be worse by his coming out with a full disclosure of all that he knew. He then stated many particulars, that had come to his own knowledge, proving a much wider diffusion of the plot than, at that period, was imagined; and, after giving up the names of several of his comrades, he mentioned the conversation which had been commenced and broken off, in the common ward of the Work House, between Monday Gell and himself. As Monday, at this period, did not seem disposed to make any confessions to others, whatever he might be inclined to do to his friend Charles, it was considered important, that the conversation between them should be renewed, and they were brought together in the same cell and left for twenty-four hours alone; but some little stratagem was employed to divert the suspicions of Monday, that Charles was confined with him, merely for the purpose of getting information out of him.

On the morning of the 10th, the Court were apprised generally of these new disclosures which Charles had made, but as he was still closeted with Monday, he could not be examined on that day, and the Court met and adjourned from day to day until the 13th; on which day Monday Gell's own confession was heard by them. Between the 10th and 13th, Charles and Monday were separated (having been respited by His Excellency, the Governor, at the request of the Court) and Charles, on his re-examination afforded much important information, which he had derived from Monday. On Monday's having all this brought to his view, he confessed his own guilt, as well as the truth of the statements which he had made to Charles. With the information obtained from Charles, arrests recommenced on the 10th, in the course of which day Peirault belonging to Mr. Strohecker was arrested; whose additional information, with some further details obtained from Harry, belonging to Mr. Haig, in conjunction with the disclosures of Charles and Monday, caused the arrest of upwards of sixty slaves in the course of three or four days. After the trial of these, and a few more subsequently arrested, the civil authorities conceiving that enough had been done to serve as an example, determined to pursue the investigation no further; but should any further information be communicated to them, to bring to trial such only as had taken an active part, and arrange with the owners of the others to send them out of the state.

By the timely discovery of this plot, South Carolina has been rescued from the most horrible catastrophe with which it has been threatened since it has been an independent state; for although success could not possibly have attended the conspirators, yet before their suppression, Charleston would probably have been wrapped in flames—many valuable lives have been sacrificed—and an immense loss of property sustained by the citizens, even though no other distressing occurrences were experienced by them; while the plantations in the lower country would have been disorganized, and the agricultural interests have sustained an enormous loss.

MEMORANDUM.

A gentleman of respectability, the owner of one of the slaves deeply engaged in the conspiracy, stated to the Court, previously to his servant's guilt being ascertained, that he was a Negro in whose honesty and veracity he confided, and whose attachment and fidelity to him had been great. This Negro had been twice in the Northern States with him, where he had every reason to believe that attempts were made to induce this slave not to return to Charleston. He further said he had owned him since 1806 or 1807, during all which time he had behaved himself well. It thus appears that even a servant whose attachment to his owner was so great that he refused to avail himself of the means of lawfully attaining his freedom (the laws of the State, or the friendly feelings of its inhabitants, where he then was putting that in his power), could not resist the arguments or threats of the conspirators, even though he knew that they aimed at nothing less than the murder of his master and family.

THE TRIALS

The Court organized for the trial of sundry Negroes apprehended and charged *with attempting to raise an Insurrection amongst the Blacks against the Whites,* and of such others as might be brought before them on the same charge, met on Wednesday, the 19th June, 1822, and consisted of the following Gentlemen, viz.:

LIONEL H. KENNEDY, Q. U. ⎫
THOMAS PARKER, J. P. ⎬ *Magistrates.*

WILLIAM DRAYTON, ⎫
NATHAN HEYWARD, ⎪
JAMES R. PRINGLE, ⎬ *Freeholders.*
JAMES LEGARE, ⎪
ROBERT J. TUMBULL, ⎭

THE TRIAL OF ROLLA, a Negro man, the slave of His Excellency, Governor Bennett—Jacob Axson, Esq., attending as counsel for his owner.

Evidence

WITNESS NO. 1[11] A Negro man testified as follows: I know Rolla, belonging to Mr. Thomas Bennett, we are intimate friends; all that I know of the intended Insurrection I got from him. About three months ago he asked me to join with him in slaying the whites, I asked him to give me time to consider it; a week after he put the same question to me, and at the end of another week he again came to me on the same subject. I told him "take care, God says we must not kill"; you are a coward he said and laughed at me. He said he would tell me how it was to be done. There are said he, white men who have come from off, and who say that Santo Domingo and Africa will assist us to get our liberty if we will only make the motion first. I advised him to let it alone, and told him I would oppose them if they came to kill my owner, when he again laughed at me as a coward. He summoned me to go to their meetings where said he you will hear what is going on and be better informed; I told him yes, I would go. Friday night about three weeks ago he appointed to take me with him to their meeting; at that night he came to me and again summoned me to go to the meeting, I went away from him, I went out of his way. The next day he came to me and said the meeting had been expecting me and I must send my name to be put down as one of the band—this thing has been going on for four months. He told me that at the meeting it was said that *some white men said Congress had set us free, and that our white people here would not let us be so,* and that Santo Domingo and Africa would come over and cut up the white people if we only made the motion here first—that last Saturday night (the 15th June) might be the last he had to live, as they were determined to break open the thing on Sunday night (the 16th June). I told him it could not be done, it would not succeed, that our parents for generations back had been slaves, and we had better be contented. He desired me to tell Witness No. 2 to go up to him, that he wished to see him. No. 2 went in the evening —Rolla told No. 2 in my presence what he was going to do—No. 2 told him to let it alone, he would not succeed, and then turned away and wept. *Rolla replied 'tis now gone too far to stop it.* He told No. 2 to go out of town on Sunday night, as he did not wish him to be hurt—I told No. 2 to sound the alarm, and if he did not I would. I asked Rolla what was to be done with the women and children? he said, *"when we have done with the fellows, we know what to do with the wenches."* He said *there are a great many involved in it in the country;* that Mungo from James' Island was to come over to Charleston with 4,000 men, land on South Bay, march up and seize the Arsenal by the Guard House and kill all the City Guard; that another body was to seize upon the Powder Magazine, and another body to take the United States' Arsenal on the Neck,

then march to town and destroy the inhabitants, who could only
escape by jumping into the river. *My Army he said will first fix my
old buck and then the Intendant.* I asked him if he could bind his
master or kill him; he laughed at me again; I then told him I
would have nothing to do with him. He said he was going to John's
Island to hasten down the country Negroes, as he feared they
would not come. I felt that it was a bad thing to disclose what a
bosom friend had confided to me, and that it was wicked to betray
him, and I suffered a great deal before I could bring myself to give
information, but when I thought on the other hand that by doing
so I would save so many lives *and prevent the horrible acts in contemplation,* 'twas overbalanced, and my duty was to inform. I refused to go to the meetings as Rolla wished, as I feared if I
opposed them there, they might make away with me to prevent me
from betraying them. I don't know where the meetings were held,
but believe 'twas in Bull Street, in which street Denmark Vesey
lives. Rolla said that Ned and Mathias were concerned. I am well
acquainted with Stephen, Mr. T. R. Smith's man; I believe him
to be a worthy, good man, and in a conversation with him on this
subject, he agreed with me that this was an abominable plot—I
have not seen him for the last four weeks. I know Denmark Vesey
—I was one day on horseback going to market when I met him on
foot; he asked me if I was satisfied in my present situation; if I
remembered the fable of Hercules and the Waggoner whose waggon was stalled, and he began to pray, and Hercules said, you fool
put your shoulder to the wheel, whip up the horses and your waggon will be pulled out; that if we did not put our hand to the work
and deliver ourselves, we should never come out of slavery; *that
Congress had made us free.* I know that he is intimately acquainted with Rolla—Rolla told me that there had been a sort of
disagreement and confusion at their place of meeting, and that they
meant to meet at Vesey's. Vesey told me that a large army from
Santo Domingo and Africa were coming to help us, and we must
not stand with our hands in our pockets; he was bitter towards the
whites. Sambo who lives on Mrs. La Roache's plantation (on
John's Island) sent word down to Rolla that he would be in town
on Sunday night last. Rolla said that they would have a counter-
sign to be known to their friends, and in the action, those blacks

who could not give it would be killed; that they would fire the town. Rolla's threats are that if any black person is found out giving information or evidence against them, they would be watched for day and night and be certainly killed. Even now the friends of those in prison are trying about the streets to find out who has given information—*If my name was known I would certainly be killed.* I advised Rolla to let it alone, but told him that if they persevered and commenced it (I had no arms), but that as they passed by my house, I would fall in behind with my fishing line and grains which was all that I had. Rolla did not tell to No. 2, all the particulars, but told him of the intended rising and the time.

WITNESS NO. 2.[12] A Negro man testified as follows: The first I heard was from witness No. 1—he told me that such was the idea of the colored people, that he was asked to join but that he asked for time to consider; that he was told to tell me to go out of town, that at twelve o'clock on Sunday (the 16th June) the rising would take place. I told him I would tell my master and he said he would do the same. On Friday (the 14th of June) witness No. 1, and myself told my master everything. I went up to Rolla as he requested, and saw him, who complained of his hard living; I found that he was at something wrong and my heart got so full that I wept. Rolla never told me in express words that he was going to join in the rising to kill the whites. Witness No. 1, was present when Rolla and myself were speaking and heard most of what passed; Rolla's last words were " *'tis gone too far now to be stopped.*" Though Rolla said nothing expressly to me about Insurrection, yet we seemed to understand each other perfectly, and that such was in contemplation. Rolla told me that on Sunday evening I must go out of town as he did not wish me to be hurt; he said words to the effect that he was going to join in the rising; he said that on Sunday night at twelve o'clock such and such a thing would take place. Witness No. 1, said that Rolla had told him they were to join and take the Powder Magazine and the Arsenal on the Neck, and that an army of 4,000 men from James' Island would land at South Bay, march up and take the Laboratory in town and kill all the City Guard, and then they would kill the whites. Witness No. 1, and Stephen, Mr. T. R. Smith's man are truly good men.

THE OWNER OF WITNESS NO. 2 testified as follows: What my

servant has just said is substantially what he told me some days ago; he is a servant of the very best character, and every word he says may be relied on. I never heard a complaint against him from white or black.

WITNESS NO. 6, a Negro man belonging to His Excellency Governor Bennett, gave the following evidence: Rolla proposed to me to join with the blacks to rise against the whites, 'twas on last Saturday (the 25th of June); he asked me to join him to raise an army against the whites; I refused and went away; he said I was a fool.

WITNESS NO. 7, a Negro man gave the following evidence: I reside on John's Island. About a month ago Rolla advised me to join the blacks against the whites, I told him it was vain; he told me to come to town on Saturday week last (the 15th of June). He said he would let me know what day to be down and sent me word last Friday week not to come down on the Saturday as the thing had been found out. He said the plan was to take the Guard House and the Magazine and then get arms and ammunition, that a great many were concerned but no name was mentioned to me. I mentioned it to no one on the Island.

The voluntary confession of Rolla[13] to the Court, made after all the evidence had been heard, but before his conviction: I know Denmark Vesey. On one occasion he asked me what news, I told him none; he replied we are free but the white people here won't let us be so, and the only way is to rise up and fight the whites. I went to his house one night to learn where the meetings were held. I never conversed on this subject with Batteau or Ned— Vesey told me he was the leader in this plot. I never conversed either with Peter or Mingo. Vesey induced me to join; when I went to Vesey's house there was a meeting there, the room was full of people, but none of them white. That night at Vesey's we determined to have arms made, and each man put in $12\frac{1}{2}$ cents towards that purpose. Though Vesey's room was full I did not know one individual there. At this meeting Vesey said we were to take the Guard House and Magazine to get arms; that we ought to rise up and fight against the whites for our liberties; he was the first to rise up and speak, and he read to us from the Bible, how the Children of Israel were delivered out of Egypt from bondage. He said that the rising would take place, last Sunday night week, (the 16th June) and that Peter Poyas was one.

On behalf of Rolla, five Witnesses were introduced and examined prior to his confession to the Court, with a view to impeach the credibility of witness No. 1, but they rather strengthened it. The owner of that witness (No. 1) who was introduced as a witness on behalf of Rolla, among other things creditable to that witness, stated, that since he had given information against Rolla, he had been distracted, that being the first day he seemed composed; that he thought and said he had acted like a traitor to his friend.

THE COURT unanimously found Rolla guilty. After sentence of death[14] had been passed upon him, he made a confession in prison to the Rev. Dr. Hall, who furnished the Court with it in writing, and in the following words: "I was invited by Denmark Vesey to his house, where I found Ned Bennett, Peter Poyas, and others, some were strangers to me, they said they were from the country. Denmark told us, it was high time we had our liberty, and he could show us how we might obtain it. He said, we must unite together as the Santo Domingo people did, never to betray one another, and to die before we would tell upon one another. He also said, he expected the Santo Domingo people would send some troops to help us. The best way, said he, for us to conquer the whites, is to set the town on fire in several places, at the Governor's Mills, and near the Docks, and for every servant in the yards to be ready with axes, knives, and clubs, to kill every man as he came out when the bells began to ring. *He then read in the Bible where God commanded, that all should be cut off, both men, women and children, and said, he believed, it was no sin for us to do so, for the Lord had commanded us to do it.* But if I had read these Psalms, Doctor, which I have read, since I have been in this prison, they would never have got me to join them. At another meeting, some of the company were opposed to killing the Ministers, and the women and children, but Denmark said, it was not safe to keep one alive, but to destroy them totally, for you see, said he, the Lord has commanded it. When I heard this, master Hall, my heart pained me within, and I said to myself, I cannot kill my master and mistress, for they use me, more like a son, than a slave. I then concluded in my mind, that I would go into the country, on Saturday evening, before they were to commence on Sunday, that I might not see it. Some of the company asked, if they were to stay in Charleston; he said no, as soon as they could get the money from the banks, and the goods from the stores, they should hoist sail for Santo Domingo, for he expected some armed vessels would meet them to conduct and protect them."

[*Note.* Every possible care was taken by the Court throughout the trials, to prevent collusion between the witnesses, or either of them knowing what the others had testified to. Those in prison were confined in different rooms, or when, from their being wanted in Court it was necessary to bring them in the room adjoining that in which the Court was sitting, they were put together in one room, a confidential noncommissioned officer of the City Guard was placed in the room with them to prevent their communicating together. They were brought in and examined separately, none of them knowing against whom they were called, until they entered the Court Room; and the evidence given in the one room could not be heard in the next. Those who were not arrested, as they could not know who were to be the witnesses against a particular individual, or what individual was to be tried, could not well collude together.]

THE TRIAL OF BATTEAU, a Negro man, the slave of His Excellency Governor Bennett—Jacob Axson, Esq. attending as counsel for the owner.

Evidence

WITNESS NO. 3 [15] A Negro, about 18 years of age testified as follows: I know Batteau, he belongs to Mr. Bennett. Sunday before last he met, stopped me and told me something very grievous—he asked me if I would go as one of the army. I told him I could not, as I was so bound to my father that I could not go out without his leave. Nothing more then took place as I immediately left him. I have not seen him since. (Cross-examined) Batteau told me this army was to raise the blacks against the whites—he said the army was to act last Sunday night (the 16th June)—before he commenced speaking to me he took me one side and then spoke low to me. My brother (witness No. 4) and myself afterwards spoke together on this business, and he said that Batteau had likewise spoken to him about it.

WITNESS NO. 4 [16] A Negro about 20 years of age gave the following evidence: I know Batteau, he belongs to Mr. Bennett. He once said to me that he wanted me to agree to join them with as many blacks as I could get to kill the whites—this was last Sunday week in the afternoon after Church. I said I could not attempt such a thing. He tried to persuade me to join but I refused—he said he could raise armies directly, that he was one at the head, that they would put one force at the Bridge and another in town, that he expected some aid from the country. The last time I saw witness, No. 3, was last Saturday night. Batteau said the rising would be last Sunday night (the 16th June). (Cross-examined.) On the Sunday afternoon I saw Batteau, 'twas near the Rev. Mr. Bachman's not far from Cannon's Bridge, he was talking with a woman. He called to me and took me to one side and began the conversation, speaking low so that no one could hear him. He said if I could raise men enough 'twixt Saturday and Sunday next to meet him to kill the white people. He said they could get arms enough. He is called Batteau and Botteau. My brother (witness No. 3) and myself afterwards spoke together on this subject, and he said that Batteau had spoken to him too.

THE COURT unanimously found Batteau guilty, and on the 28th June passed upon him the sentence of death.

On the first day of July, the following letter was received from His Excellency Governor Bennett:

Charleston, July 1st, 1822.

L. H. KENNEDY, ESQ. Q. U.

THOS. PARKER, J. P.

Presiding Magistrates of the Court of Justices and Freeholders organized for the trial of slaves charged with attempting to raise an insurrection:

Gentlemen:

After a very attentive consideration of the evidence yesterday presented, permit me to request that the case of Batteau may be reviewed with a view to the mitigation of his punishment; such a power is vested in the Court by the provisions of the act for the better ordering and governing of slaves.

If guilty of an attempt to raise an insurrection, it does not appear from the evidence to extend beyond an invitation to two boys to join in the project: from no part of the evidence does it appear that he is further implicated.

It is known that one of the boys referred to, was charged with using improper threats, and therefore supposed to be involved in the general plot, for which he was arrested. As he states that he had subsequently a communication with his brother, and they both testify to a simple isolated fact, collusion may be inferred. And even admitting the truth of their evidence, it would not appear that he is equally guilty with the others. If so the benignant provisions of that act would sanction the request made.

I ask this Gentlemen, as an individual incurring a severe and distressing loss.

I am very respectfully,
Your obedient serv't,
THOMAS BENNETT

THE COURT agreeable to the request contained in the above letter, reviewed their decision, but after having sent for and again interrogated witness Nos. 3 and 4, came unanimously to the conclusion they had at first done. After his execution it was incidentally proved, in the course of the subsequent trials, that he attended the meetings of the conspirators at Vesey's.

STEPHEN, a Negro man belonging to Mr. Thomas R. Smith, was next brought before the Court, but there being no testimony against him, he was immediately discharged.

THE TRIAL OF PETER, a Negro man, the property of Mr. James Poyas—Mr. Poyas with Robert Bentham, Esq. as his counsel attending.

Evidence
WITNESS NO. 5 [17] A Negro man gave the following evidence: I know Peter, he belongs to Mr. James Poyas. In May last Peter

and myself met in Legare Street, at the corner of Lambol Street, when the following conversation took place. He asked me the news —I replied none that I know of. He said by George we can't live so—I replied how will we do. He said we can do very well; if you can find anyone to assist us will you join. I asked him how do you mean—he said, why to break the yoke. I replied I don't know. He asked me suppose you were to hear that the whites were going to kill you would you defend yourself—I replied I'd try to escape. He asked have you lately seen Denmark Vesey, and has he spoken to you particularly—I said no. Well then said he that's all now, but call at the shop tomorrow after knocking off work and I will tell you more—we then parted. I met him the next day according to appointment, when he said to me, we intend to see if we can't do something for ourselves, we can't live so. I asked him where he would get men—he said we'll find them fast enough, we have got enough—we expect men from country and town. But how said I will you manage it—why we will give them notice said he, and they will march down and camp round the city. But what said I will they do for arms—he answered they will find arms enough, they will bring down their hoes, axes, &c. I said that won't do to fight with here—he said stop, let us get candidates from town with arms, and we will then take the Guard House and Arsenal in town, the Arsenal on the Neck and the upper Guard House, and supply the country people with arms. How said I will you approach these Arsenals for they are guarded—yes said he, I know that, but what are those guards, one man here and one man there, we won't let a man pass before us. Well said I but how will the black people from the country and those from the Islands know when you are to begin; or how will you get the town people together—why said he we will have *prayer meetings at night and there notify them* when to start and as the clock strikes 12 all must move—But said I, the whites in the back country, Virginia, when they hear the news will turn to and kill you all, and besides you may be betrayed. Well said he what of that, if one gets hanged we will rise at that minute. We then left his shop and walked towards Broad Street, when he said *I want you to take notice of all the shops and stores in town with arms in them, take down the numbers and give them to me.* I said I will see to it and then we parted. About the 1st June

I saw in the public papers a statement that the white people were going to build Missionary Houses for the blacks, which I carried and showed to Peter and said to him, you see the good they are going to do for us—when he said, what of that, have you not heard that on the 4th July the whites are going to create a false alarm of fire, and every black that comes out will be killed in order to thin them. Do you think that they would be so barbarous said I. Yes said he I do; I fear they have knowledge of an army from Santo Domingo, and they would be right to do it, to prevent us from joining that army if it should march towards this land. I was then very much alarmed—we then parted and I saw no more of him until (the Guards were very strict) about a fortnight ago. At that time I saw Peter and Ned Bennett standing and talking together at the corner of Lambol and Legare Streets—they crossed over and met me by Mrs. Myles, and Ned Bennett said to me, did you hear what those boys were taken up for the other day. I replied No, but some say 'twas for stealing. Ned asked me if I was sure I had never said anything to the whites about what Peter Poyas had spoken to me about—I replied No—says Peter you never did—No I answered—says Ned to me how do you stand—at which I struck the tree box with my knuckles and said, as firm as this box, I'll never say one word against you. Ned then smiled and nodded his head and said, that will do, when we all separated. Last Tuesday or Wednesday week Peter said to me you see my lad how the white people have got to windward of us—you won't said I be able to do anything. O yes said he we will, by George we are obliged to—he said all down this way ought to meet and have a collection to purchase powder. What said I is the use of powder, the whites can fire three times to our once—he said but 'twill *be such a dead time of night they won't know what is the matter, and our Horse Companies will go about the streets and prevent the whites from assembling.* I asked him where will you get horses—why said he there are many butcher boys with horses, and there are the public Livery Stables, where we have several candidates and the waiting men belonging to the white people of the Horse Companies will be told to take away their master's horses. He asked me if my master was not a horseman—I said yes. Has he not got arms in his house—I answered yes. Can't they be got at—I said yes—then

said he 'tis good to have them. I asked him what was the plan—
why said he after we have taken the Arsenal and Guard Houses,
then we will set the town on fire in different places, and as the
whites come out we will slay them; if we were to set fire to the
town first, the man in the steeple would give the alarm too soon—
*I am the Captain said he, to take the lower Guard House and
Arsenal.* But, I replied, when you are coming up the sentinel will
give the alarm—he said he would advance a little distance ahead,
and if he could only get a *grip at his throat he was a gone man,* for
his sword was very sharp; he had sharpened it and had made it
so sharp it had cut his finger, which he showed me. As to the
Arsenal on the Neck he said that is gone as sure as fate, *Ned
Bennett would manage that with the people from the country, and
the people between Hibben's Ferry and Santee would land and
take the upper Guard House.* I then said, then this thing seems
true. My man, said he, God has a hand in it, we have been meeting
for four years and are not yet betrayed. I told him I was afraid
after all of the white people from the back country and Virginia.
He said that the blacks would collect so numerous *from the country*
we need not fear the whites from other parts, for when we have
once got the city we can keep them all out. He asked if I had told
my boys—I said no—then said he you should do it, for Ned Bennett has his people pretty well ranged; but said he take care and
don't mention it to those waiting men who receive *presents of old
coats from their masters or they'll betray us;* I will speak to them.
We then parted and I have not since conversed with him. He said
the rising was to take place last Sunday night (16th June)—*that
any of the colored people who said a word about this matter would
be killed by the others—the little man who can't be killed, shot, or
taken* is named Jack, a Gullah Negro. Peter said there was a
French company in town *of* 300 *men fully armed*—that he was to
see Monday Gell about expediting the rising. I know that Mingo
went often to Mr. Paul's to see Edwin, but don't know if he spoke
with William. *Peter said he had a sword* and I ought to get one—
he said he had a letter from the country, I think from St. Thomas',
from a Negro man who belonged to the Captain of a Militia Company, who said he could easily get the key of the house where the
Company's arms were put after muster, and take them all out and

help in that way. This business originates altogether with the *African Congregation* in which Peter is a leader. When Bennett's Ned asked about those taken up, he alluded particularly to Mr. Paul's William, and asked me if I had said anything to him about it.

THE OWNER OF WITNESS NO. 5, testified as follows: My servant bears a good character. His general conduct is good. He was raised up in my family, and I would place my life in his hands.

WILLIAM, a Negro man belonging to Mr. Paul, testified as follows: Mr. Harth's Negro man Mingo told me about the insurrection and referred me to Peter Poyas for further information, who he said had a list with 9,000 names upon it, and that he was still taking down names. On the week I was to see Peter I was apprehended. Mingo said that 600 men on the Bay were already down on the list in Peter's possession. I never had any conversation with Peter. Peter, Ned Bennett, and Charles Shubrick are *class leaders in the African Church.* The African Association have also a church in Anson Street and one in Cow Alley, where they have service. Mingo said that Peter would tell me when the rising would take place. He said that letters were passing between Peter Poyas, Ned Bennett, and Charles Shubrick, and that all the orders he got, he got from Peter. My fellow servant Edwin brought the first news of the rising into our yard. He has a wife at Mr. Parker's near the lines. One Monday morning when he came from his wife's he told me there would be something shortly between the blacks and the whites—that he knew the parties and that the thing was going on, and *all the African Church were engaged in it,* and in particular mentioned Peter Poyas and Ned Bennett. Edwin told me generally about the matter—that Peter knew all, and that all who wants to know goes to him.

Rolla in his confession said, that Denmark Vesey told him Peter was one.

THE COURT unanimously found Peter guilty, and passed upon him the sentence of death.

Subsequently to Peter's trial, a good deal of testimony was given against him in the course of the succeeding trials. Among others, witness No. 10 testified that Peter Poyas was the first man who spoke to me and asked me to join. I asked him what, the

Church—he said no, have you not heard that the blacks were joining to try to take the country. I asked him if he thought he had
men enough to do it—he said yes, a plenty of men and the society
will contribute money with which a white man would purchase
guns and powder for them. He said he would call back, and I must
consider if I would join them. He called back and asked me if I
was willing now—why Peter said I you have not got force enough.
He said if I did not join he would turn all my country people
against me—said I, if so, I'll join you, but you must not put my
name down, when you come out if I find you strong enough I'll
join you. Well said he if you don't join you'll be killed. Peter and
Harry Haig called on me afterwards—I was not at home. Peter
Poyas told me also that they had force enough, that some would
come from James' Island and John's Island, and some from Christ
Church Parish, where he generally went over to a meeting to have
a talk, and that he had some about and in town, the number of
which he would show me from the Society Books if I would only
come to the Society. He said they were to fight the whites and keep
on fighting 'til the English came to help them—Harry Taig told
me the same thing. (See also Frank Ferguson's testimony against
Denmark Vesey, who told him that "himself, Ned, Peter, and
Monday Gell were the principal men, and himself the head man.")

THE TRIAL OF AMHERST, a Negro man belonging to Mrs.
Lining. The strongest part of the testimony against him was, his
requesting his class leader on Sunday, the 16th June to pray for
him, as it might be the last day he had to live. Amherst admitted
that he had said so, and that he alluded to the intended insurrection, which he had that day heard of; but denied that he was in
any manner engaged in it, and only asked for the prayers of his
class leader, as in the confusion, he would be in danger of losing
his life whether he was engaged in it or not.

THE COURT *unanimously* found him not guilty and discharged
him.

THE TRIAL OF NED, a Negro man the slave of His Excellency
Governor Bennett—Jacob Axson, Esq. attending as counsel for
his owner.

Evidence

WITNESS NO. 5, testified as follows: About the 7th June I saw Peter and Ned Bennett standing and talking together at the corner of Lambol and Legare Streets—they crossed over and met me by Mrs. Myles, and Ned Bennett said to me, did you hear what those boys were taken up for the other day—I replied No, but some say 'twas for stealing. Ned asked me if I was sure I had never said anything to the whites about what Peter Poyas had spoken to me about—I replied No—says Peter you never did—No I answered—says Ned to me how do you stand—at which I struck the tree box with my knuckles and said, as firm as this box, I'll never say one word against you—Ned then smiled and nodded his head and said, that will do, when we all separated. Peter told me that Ned Bennett with the people *from the country* would attack and take the Arsenal on the Neck. He asked me if I had told my boys—I said no—then said he you should do it; for Ned Bennett has his people pretty well ranged. When Ned Bennett asked about those taken up, he alluded particularly to Mr. Paul's William, and asked me if I had said anything to him about it.

WILLIAM, Mr. Paul's Slave testified as follows: Mingo Harth told me that Ned Bennett knew all about it, and told it all to Mr. Bennett's people, and that letters were passing between Peter Poyas, Ned Bennett, and Charles Shubrick, and that Ned Bennett and Charles Shubrick were officers. My fellow servant Edwin told me he knew the parties and that the thing was going on well—that all the African Congregation were engaged in it and Peter Poyas and Ned Bennett.

WITNESS NO. 1, testified that Rolla said Ned and Mathias were concerned.

FRANK, A NEGRO MAN, the slave of Mrs. Ferguson, gave the following evidence: Vesey told me that Ned Bennett and Peter Poyas were concerned with him, and that they were to go about and tell the blacks that they were free and must rise and fight for themselves. He said that himself, Ned Bennett, Peter Poyas, and Monday Gell were the principal men, and himself the head man—that they were the principal men to go about and inform the people, and fix them. I have seen Ned Bennett at Vesey's—I met Ned

Bennett, Monday Gell, and others at Vesey's, where they were talking about this business.

THE COURT unanimously found Ned guilty, and passed upon him the sentence of death.

Jesse in his confession to the Rev. Dr. Hall said, "at another meeting at Denmark Vesey's, Ned Bennett and Peter Poyas and several others were present, and in conversation about this business."

THE TRIAL OF JESSE, a Negro man, the slave of Mr. Thomas Blackwood—his owner attending.

Evidence

SALLY, a Negro woman, the slave of Mr. Alexander Howard, gave the following evidence: I know Jesse and heard him speak several times about it. One day in particular he was anxious to see his brother who has my mother for his wife, and waited until he came, when they conversed together. Jesse said he had got a horse *to go into the country to bring down men* to fight the white people, that he was allowed to pass by two parties of the patrol on the road, but that a third party had brought him back, and that if there were but five men like him they would destroy the city—this was on last Sunday week (the 16th June). He said that before 3 o'clock on that night all the white people would be killed—that if any person informed or would not join in the fight, such person would be killed or poisoned. He frequently came into the yard to see his brother, and I threatened to inform if he came there and spoke in that way to get us all into trouble. We never had any quarrel.

LOT, a Negro man, the slave of Mr. Forrester, testified as follows: I know Jesse—he met me last Sunday week (16th June) at the corner of Boundary Street, as I was coming into town. He said he was going to get a horse *to go into the country.* From what my master had told me the Thursday before I distrusted his errand and gave him something of a caution when I was going down into town towards Mr. Hibben's Ferry Slip and conversing with him— he said *you shall see tonight when I come down what I am going up for, and if my own father does not assist I will cut off his head.*

He said he was going *as far as Goose Creek Bridge,* and would get him a horse if it cost him nine dollars—the church bells were then ringing, and at half past ten o'clock the same day I saw him at Mr. Howard's, and afterwards *understood from Sally that he had set off for the country and had been brought down by the Patrol.*

SYKE, a Negro man, the slave of Mr. Waring, gave the following testimony: Jesse asked me on Sunday week last (16th June), before breakfast, where he could get a horse to go a little way *into the country.* I told him I did not know—he then went away and did not return before nine o'clock that night—he had a wife at Mr. Waring's.

FRANK, Mrs. Ferguson's slave, testified as follows: On the 15th of June, Vesey gave $2 to Jesse to hire a horse *to go into the country to my Mistress' plantation in St. John's, to inform the people to be down* on the night of the 16th. Myself and Adam put in 25 cents each for it. Vesey told Jesse, if he could not go, he must send someone else.

The voluntary confession of Jesse to the Court, made after all the evidence had been heard, but before his conviction.

I have had several conversations with Denmark Vesey, the first about four weeks ago (about 1st June) he asked me if I had heard about the rising, and did I know that the colored people were going to try to get their liberty. I then could stop no longer and he asked me to call and see him. I afterwards met him on Wednesday previous to the Sunday (16th of June) that the rising was to take place—we walked up St. Philip Street and were joined by Frank Ferguson opposite Liberty Street, and we all three walked up to Vesey's house. Says Frank I am just from the country—well says Vesey and what success—says Frank I have got two fine men for our purpose on my Mistress' plantation, who must be sent up to and informed when the people are wanted in town. Vesey asked me if I would be the man to go—I said yes, but I don't know the way—says Vesey, Frank will tell you. Frank then told me how to go to Mrs. Ferguson's plantation, and that I must ask for John O and Pompey and gave me other directions. Vesey then gave me $2 to hire a horse and Frank and Adam threw down on the table 25 cents each, I don't know what for. This was

about one o'clock on Saturday before last (15th June)—I promised to go that night. On Sunday I met Lot who betrayed me; the
same day I told Vesey I had started but that the Patrol turned me
back; in fact I had not started and only told him so to deceive him.
The same day I met Charles Drayton at Vesey's who said the business was postponed. Vesey asked Charles how he knew the business
was postponed—Charles said Ned Bennett and Monday Gell told
him so. But said Vesey, how could they know it was postponed as
they have not seen me—says Charles, they said they had seen you
and that you had told them so. Now, said I to Vesey, you see there,
suppose I had gone into the country and brought those people
down tonight, we should all have been destroyed. As far as I
know, I believe *Denmark Vesey and Monday Gell were the chief
men.*

THE COURT unanimously found Jesse guilty, and passed upon
him the sentence of death.

Subsequently to his conviction, he made the following confession in prison *to the Rev. Dr. Hall*—I was invited to Denmark
Vesey's house, and when I went, I found several men together,
among them was Ned Bennett, Peter Poyas, and others whom I
did not know. Denmark opened the meeting by saying, he had an
important secret to communicate to us, which we must not disclose
to anyone, and if we did, we should be put to instant death. He
said we were deprived of our rights and privileges by the white
people, and that our Church was shut up so that we could not use
it, and that it was high time for us to seek for our rights, and that
we were fully able to conquer the whites, if we were only unanimous and courageous, as the Santo Domingo people were. He then
proceeded to explain his plan, by saying that they intended to make
the attack by setting the Governor's Mills on fire, and also some
houses near the water, and as soon as the bells began to ring for
fire, that they should kill every man as he came out of his door, and
that the servants in the yard should do it, and that it should be
done with axes and clubs, and afterwards they should murder the
women and children, for he said, God had so commanded it in the
Scriptures. At another meeting at Denmark's, Ned Bennett, Peter
Poyas, and several others were present. In conversation some said

they thought it was cruel to kill the ministers, and the women and children, but Denmark Vesey said, *he thought it was for our safety not to spare one white skin alive, for this was the plan they pursued in Santo Domingo*. He then said to me, Jesse, I want you to go into the country to enlist as many of the country Negroes as possible, to be in readiness to come down to assist us. I told him I had no horse and no money to hire one; he then took out two dollars, and gave them to me to hire a horse, and told me to enlist as many as possible. I got the horse the next Sabbath and started, but the guard was so strict I could not pass them without being taken up. So I returned and told Denmark, at which he expressed his sorrow, and said the business was urgent for they wanted the country people to be armed, that they might attack the forts at the same time, and also to take every ship and vessel in the harbor, and to put every man to death except the Captains. Because said he, it will not be safe to stay in Charleston, for as soon as they had all the money out of the banks, and the goods out of the stores on board, they intended to sail for Santo Domingo, for he had a promise that they would receive and protect them.

This Jesse asserted to me, was the truth, whilst the tears were running down his cheeks, and he appeared truly penitent, and I have reason to hope, that he obtained pardon from God, through the merits of Christ, and was prepared to meet his fate with confidence and that he was accepted of God. At four o'clock, on the morning of the execution, I visited all the prisoners condemned, and found Jesse at prayers. He told me, his mind was placid and calm; he then assured me, that what he had told me was the truth, and that he was prepared to meet his God.

THE TRIAL OF SAMUEL GUIFFORD, a free Negro, and *ROBERT HADDEN,* a free mulatto; both of them boys.

Evidence

JOHN WOODWORTH, a white boy, testified as follows: I am 14 years old. About a week ago (subsequent to the 16th June), I heard Robert Hadden say to Samuel Guifford, he was going to join to set fire to the town, take the Magazine, and kill every white man who did not give up the country. I do not think he meant me to hear him. Robert Herron, Jefferson Campbell, and Henry Woodworth were also present.

ROBERT HERRON, a white boy deposed as follows: I am 12 years old. I heard Robert Hadden say, that on the night they raised they would kill the Governor, fire the Magazine, and kill every damn white man who would not give up the country to the Blacks. He spoke moderately loud, and did not seem to care who heard him. Samuel Guifford afterwards repeated to me what Hadden had said.

THE COURT were satisfied that the expressions charged had been used by the prisoners, but from their youth and other circumstances, they considered them rather as the effect of puerile boasting, than as evidencing a conspiracy on their part. The prisoners were therefore *unanimously found* not guilty, *but ordered* to be retained in custody *charged with a minor offence.* They were afterwards whipped in the Work House and discharged.

MATHIAS, the slave of Governor Bennett; Mungo the slave of Mr. James Poyas; Richard and John, the slaves of Mr. I. Lucas; and Sandy, belonging to Mr. Holmes, were discharged by the Court as not guilty. Jim, belonging to Mr. Ancrum; and Friday, the property of Mr. Rout, were found not guilty, and discharged. Against them there was little or no testimony.

THE TRIAL OF ABRAHAM, a Negro man, the slave of Dr. Poyas—his owner attending.

Evidence

The following letter, found in the trunk of Peter Poyas, was acknowledged by Abraham, to have been written by himself:

Dear Sir:

With pleasure I give you an answer. I will endeavor to do it. Hoping that God will be in the midst to help his own. Be particular and make a sure remark. Fear not, the Lord God that delivered Daniel is able to deliver us. All that I inform agreed. I am gone up to Beach Hill.

(*Signed*)   ABRAHAM POYAS

Abraham for several days denied that the following words in that letter, viz.:—*fear not . . . all that I inform agreed*—were written by him, saying, that they must have been added by someone. This, however, was evidently false, as he himself in a day or two afterwards admitted, but not before Peter Poyas had stated to the Court that every word in the letter was there when he received it. On Peter's being asked to explain the meaning of the letter, he said, it alluded to the Negroes in Abraham's neighborhood, who had all agreed that Abraham should be permitted to change his Church and join theirs. Abraham, however, gave a different meaning to it, and said, it related to his having two wives. Dr. Poyas, however, stated to the Court, that Abraham had subsequently given to him the same explanation of the letter that Peter had done. Although this letter taken in connection with his conduct was extremely suspicious, yet there being no other testimony against Abraham, he was found not guilty.

THE TRIAL OF DENMARK VESEY, a free black man—Col. G. W. Cross attending as his counsel.

Evidence

William, the slave of Mr. Paul, testified as follows: Mingo Harth told me *that Denmark Vesey was the chief man, and more concerned than anyone else.* Denmark Vesey is an old man in whose yard my master's Negro woman Sarah cooks. He was her father-in-law, having married her mother Beck, and though they have been parted some time, yet he visited her at her house near the Intendant's (Major Hamilton), where I have often heard him speak of the rising. *He said he would not like to have a white man in his presence—that he had a great hatred for the whites,* and that if all were like him they would resist the whites. He studied all he could to put it into the heads of the blacks to have a rising against the whites, and tried to induce me to join. He tried to induce all his acquaintances—this has been his chief study and delight for a considerable time. My last conversation with him was in April. He studied the Bible a great deal and tried to prove from it that slavery and bondage is against the Bible. I am persuaded that Denmark Vesey was chiefly concerned in this business.

WITNESS NO. 1, gave the following testimony: I know Denmark Vesey. I was one day on horseback going to market when I met him on foot; he asked me if I was satisfied in my present situation; if I remembered the fable of Hercules and the Waggoner whose waggon was stalled, and he began to pray, and Hercules said, you fool put your shoulder to the wheel, whip up the horses and your waggon will be pulled out; that if we did not put our hand to the work and deliver ourselves, we should never come out of slavery; *that Congress had made us free.* I know that he is intimately acquainted with Rolla—Rolla told me that there had been a sort of disagreement and confusion at their place of meeting, and that they meant to meet at Vesey's. Vesey told me that a large army from Santo Domingo and Africa were coming to help us, and we must not stand with our hands in our pockets; he was bitter towards the whites. (See the confessions of Rolla on pages 46–47.)

FRANK, Mrs. Ferguson's slave gave the following evidence: I know Denmark Vesey and have been to his house. I have heard him say that the Negro's situation was so bad he did not know how they could endure it, and was astonished they did not rise and fend for themselves, and he advised me to join and rise. He said he was going about to see different people, and mentioned the names of Ned Bennett and Peter Poyas as concerned with him—that he had spoken to Ned and Peter on this subject, and that they were to go about and tell the blacks that they were free, and must rise and *fight for themselves*—that they would take the Magazines and Guard Houses, and the city and be free—that he was going to send *into the country* to inform the people there too. He said he wanted me to join them—I said I could not answer—he said if I would not go into the country for him he could get others. He said himself, Ned Bennett, Peter Poyas, and Monday Gell were the principal men and himself the head man. He said they were the principal men to go about and inform the people and fix them,—that *one party would land on South Bay, one about Wappoo, and about the farms*—that the party which was to land on South Bay was to take the Guard

House and get arms and then they would be able to go on—that the attack was to commence about twelve o'clock at night—*that great numbers would come from all about,* and it must succeed as so many were engaged in it—that they would kill all the whites— that they would leave their master's houses and assemble to- gether near the lines, march down and meet the party which would land on South Bay—that he was going to *send a man into the country* on a horse *to bring down the country people* and that he would pay for the horse. He gave $2 to Jesse to get the horse on Saturday week last (15th June), about one o'clock in the day, and myself and No. 3, also put in 25 cents a piece, and he told Jesse, if he could not go he must send someone else. I have seen Ned Bennett at Vesey's. One night, I met at Vesey's a great number of men, and as they came in each handed him some money. Vesey said there was a *little man named Jack* who could not be killed, and who would furnish them with arms, he had a charm and he would lead them—that Charles Drayton had prom- ised to be engaged with them. Vesey said the Negroes were living such an abominable life, they ought to rise. I said I was living well—he said though I was, others were not and that 'twas such fools as I, that were in the way and would not help them, and that after all things were well he would mark me. He said he did not go with *Creighton to Africa, because he had not a will, he wanted to stay and see what he could do* for his fellow creatures. I met Ned, Monday, and others at Denmark Vesey's where they were talking about the business. The first time I spoke with Monday Gell 'twas one night at Denmark Vesey's house, where I heard Vesey tell Monday that he must *send someone into the country to bring the people down.* Monday said *he had sent up Jack* and told him *to tell the people to come down and join in the fight* against the whites and also to ascertain and inform him how many people he could get. A few days after I met Vesey, Monday, and Jack, in the streets under Mr. Duncan's trees at night, where *Jack stated that he had been into the country round by Goose Creek and Dorchester,* and that he had spoken to 6,600 persons who had agreed to join. Monday said to Vesey, that if Jack had so many men they had better wait no longer but begin the business at once, and others would join. The first time I saw

Monday at Vesey's, he was going away early, when Vesey asked him to stay, to which Monday replied, he expected that night a meeting at his house to fix upon and mature the plan, and that he could stay no longer. I afterwards conversed with Monday in his shop, where he asked me if I had heard that Bennett's and Poyas' people were taken up, that 'twas a great pity—he said he had joined in the business—I told him to take care he was not taken up. Whenever I talked with Vesey, he always spoke of Monday Gell as being his principal and active man in the business.

ADAM, a Negro man belonging to Mr. Ferguson testified as follows: Denmark Vesey one day asked me to walk to his house, and there asked me for 25 cents to hire a horse to send up into the country. I put down the money on the table and asked what he was going to send into the country for—he said 'twould be for my benefit. As he would tell me no more I took up the money and put it back into my pocket again. I afterwards met the man who was to go into the country, who told me he had set off, but had been brought back by the Patrol; *that he was going up to bring down the black people to take this country from the whites.* I have been at Vesey's house and there it was I met the man who was to go into the country, he was a yellowish man—the witness pointing at Jesse said, that is the man who was to go into the country. (See the confession of Jesse to the Court on pages 57–58.)

BENJAMIN FORD, a white lad, about 15 or 16 years of age, deposed as follows: Denmark Vesey frequently came into our shop which is near his house, and always complained of the hardships of the blacks. He said the laws were very rigid and strict and that the blacks had not their rights—that everyone had his time, and that his would come round too. *His general conversation was about religion which he would apply to slavery,* as for instance, he would speak of the creation of the world, in which he would say all men had equal rights, blacks as well as whites,—*all his religious remarks were mingled with slavery.*

THE COURT unanimously found Denmark Vesey guilty, and passed upon him the sentence of death. After his conviction, a good deal of testimony was given against him during the succeeding trials. Among others:

WITNESS NO. 9, a Negro man, testified as follows: Denmark Vesey has frequently spoken to me about the intended insurrection, and endeavored to persuade me to join them. He inquired of me *if my master had not arms in his house, and tried to persuade me to get them for him.* The blacks stand in great fear of him, and I so much so, that I always endeavored to avoid him.

EDWIN, a Negro man belonging to Mr. Paul, gave the following evidence: Charles Drayton told me that Denmark Vesey and Monday Gell knew about the insurrection of the blacks, and that my fellow servant *William, in consequence of what he had said, would run great risk of his life if he went out.* I have heard everybody, even the women say, when several were apprehended at first, that they wondered why Denmark Vesey and Monday Gell were not taken up. (See confession of Jesse to the Rev. Dr. Hall, on pages 58–59.)

THE TRIAL OF MONDAY, a Negro man, the slave of Mr. John Gell,—Col. Wm. Rouse as his friend, and Jacob Axson, Esq., counsel for his owner attending.

Evidence

FRANK, belonging to Mrs. Ferguson, testified as follows: The first time I spoke with Monday Gell, was one night at Vesey's house, where I heard Vesey tell Monday *he must send someone into the country to bring the people down.* Monday said *he had sent up* Jack, and told him to bring the people down, and tell them to come down and join in the fight against the whites, and to ascertain and inform him how many people he could get. A few days after, I met Vesey, Monday, and Jack in the street, under Mr. Duncan's trees at night, where Jack stated that he had been in the *country, round by Goose Creek and Dorchester,* and that he had spoken to 6,600 persons who had agreed to join. At Vesey's the first time I saw Monday, he was going away, Vesey asked him to stay, when Monday said he expected that night a meeting at his house to fix upon and mature the plan, and he could not stay. I afterwards conversed with Monday in his shop, where he asked me if I had heard that Bennett's and Poyas' people were taken up, that 'twas a great pity—he said that he had joined in the business—I told him to take care he was not taken up. Whenever I talked with Vesey he always spoke of Monday Gell as being his principal and active man in this business. I heard Gullah Jack say he would pay no more wages, he was too busy in seeing about this insurrection; besides what would the white people want with wages since they would soon be no more. Monday Gell said to Vesey, that if Jack had so many men they had better wait no longer, but begin the business at once and others would join. (See Edwin's testimony, page 65.)

WITNESS NO. 10, a Negro man gave the following evidence: I saw Charles Drayton before the 16th at Monday Gell's. I was going to market and Charles called to me as I was crossing the street. Joe, who has a wife at Mr. Remoussin's, asked me if I did not know that Monday was at the head of the Ebo Company who are going to fight the white people. Monday is an Ebo. I asked Joe if he was one of that Company—he said yes he was. I asked him what he could do as he was an invalid—he said he would take Remoussin's sword and gun and tell him to lay down in his bed and be quiet. We parted. Previous to the 16th of June, Monday Gell called me into his shop. I went in and said to him, I heard he was Captain of his countrymen's company the Ebo's—he said he was a sort of a one. I bid him good morning, when he said when you want to hear the news come here. I never saw him afterwards. Monday and Charles were very often together. (See the latter part of Jesse's confession, page 58.)

WITNESS NO. 5, testified as follows: Peter Poyas told me about the 10th of June, that he was to see Monday Gell about expediting the rising.

THE COURT unanimously found Monday guilty, and passed upon him the sentence of death, after which he made the following Confession: I come out as a man who knows he is about to die. Sometime after Christmas, Vesey passed my door, he called in and said to me that he was trying to gather the blacks to try and see if anything could be done to overcome the whites; he asked me to join; I asked him his plan and his numbers; he said he had Peter Poyas, Ned Bennett, and Jack Purcell; he asked me to join; I said no; he left me and I saw him not for sometime. About four or five weeks ago as I went up Wentworth Street, Frank Ferguson met me, and said he had four plantations of people who he was to go for on Saturday, 15th June. How, said I, will you bring them down; he said through the woods; he asked me if I was going towards Vesey's to ask Vesey to be at home that evening, and he would be there to tell me his success. I asked Jack Purcell to carry this message, he said he would; that same evening at my house I met Vesey's mulatto boy, he told me Vesey wished to see me, I went with him; when I went into Vesey's I met Ned Bennett, Peter Poyas, Frank Ferguson, Adam, and Gullah Jack; they were consulting about the plan; Frank told Vesey on Saturday 15th, he would go and bring down the people and lodge them near town in the woods; the plan was to arm themselves by breaking open the stores with arms. I then told Vesey I would join them, after sometime I told them I had some business of my own and asked them to excuse me, I went away, and only then was I ever there. One evening, Peirault Strohecker, and Bacchus Hammet brought to my shop a keg, and asked me to let it stay there till they sent for it; I said yes, but did not know the contents; the next evening Gullah Jack came and took away the keg, this was before the 16th June; since I have been in prison I learned that the keg contained powder.

Pharo Thompson is concerned, and he told me a day or two after Ned and Peter were taken up, if he could get a fifty dollar bill, he would run away. About two Sundays before I was brought here, he asked me, in Archdale Street, when shall we be like those white people in the Church. I said when it pleased God. Sunday before I was taken up, he met me as I came out of Archdale Church, and took me into a stable in said street, and told me he told his master, who had asked him, that he had nothing to do in this affair, which was a lie. William Colcock came to my shop once and said a brother told him that five hundred men were making up for the same purpose. Frank said he was to send to Hell-Hole Swamp to get men.

Peirault Strohecker is engaged; he used to go of a Sunday on horseback up the road to a man he knows on the same errand. One Sunday he asked me to go with him—I went and Smart

Anderson. We went to a small house a little way from the road after you turn into the shipyard road, on its left hand. They two went into the stable with an old man that lived there, I remained in the yard. They remained in the stable about half an hour; as soon as they came out, Peirault and I started to town to go to Church, and left Smart there. I was told by Denbow Martin, who has a wife in Mr. Smith's house, that Stephen Smith belonged to some of the gangs.

Saby Gaillard is concerned, he met me on the Bay, before the 16th June and gave me a piece of paper from his pocket; this paper was about the battle that Boyer had in Santo Domingo. In a day or two he called on me and asked if I had read it, and said if he had as many men he would do the same too, as he could whip ten white men himself. He frequently came to me to speak about this matter, and at last I had to insult him out of the shop; he and Paris Ball were often together. A week before I was taken up, Paris told me that my name was called.

Billy Palmer and Vesey were constantly together. There was once in my shop a long talk between them about this same matter; I begged them to stop it; Vesey told him to try to get as many as he could; he said he would.

John Vincent told me that Edward Johnson, a free man, had said, as he was a free man he would have nothing to do with slaves, but the night they began he would join them.

I told Charles Drayton what uproar there was about this business, and since we have been here we have talked together.

Albert Inglis came to me and asked if I knew anything about it; I said yes. He asked me if I had joined; I said yes. He said he was one also; he said Adam, a free man wanted to see me so I went with him one night. Adam asked me how many men had joined; I told him what Frank Ferguson had said. He asked me if I believed it; I said yes. He said if he could only find men behind him he would go before. Previous to the 16th, Albert said to me quit the business; I told him I was too far into it, so I must stick to it.

I never wrote to Santo Domingo or anywhere else on this subject, nor kept a list or books, nor saw any such things, but heard that Paul's William had a list, nor did I hear anything about arms being in possession of the blacks. I didn't know that Tom Russel made pikes, nor that Gullah Jack had any of them.

Lewis Remoussin called at my shop and asked me to call at his house, he had something to tell me, but I did not go; Jack Glen told me he was engaged.

I met Scipio Simms one Sunday, coming from the country, who said he had been near the Savannah's to Mr. Middleton's place; I heard afterwards that his errand was on this business.

I know John the cooper, who said he was engaged too in this business.

William Garner said he was engaged in it and had got twelve or thirteen draymen to join.

Sandy Vesey told me he belonged to it too.

At Vesey's house, Frank told Gullah Jack to put one ball and three buck shot in each cartridge.

Mingo Harth acknowledged to me that he had joined, and Peter Poyas told me so too; Mingo told me so several times; Mingo said he was to have his master's horse on the night of the 16th.

Lot Forrester told me frequently that he was one of the company, and I know that he had joined in the business myself. Isaac Harth told me once that he had joined, he knew I was in the business.

Morris Brown knew nothing of it, and we agreed not to let him, Harry Drayton, or Charles Corr know anything about it.

———— told me in my store that he was to get some powder from his master and give it to Peter Poyas; he seemed to have been a long time engaged in it, and to know a great deal. Joe Jore acknowledged to me once or twice that he had joined, he said he knew some of the Frenchmen concerned; he knew I was in it.

Subsequently to this confession, Monday was examined as a witness in a number of cases, during which, he stated many things he had not mentioned in his confession. The Court conceiving it all important to obtain from Monday all the information he possessed (believing him to possess more information on this subject than any man then alive), offered to recommend him to the Governor for a conditional pardon, or commutation of his punishment to banishment, if he would reveal all he knew in relation to this plot. He promised to do so, and made this second confession:

The first time I heard of the intended insurrection, was about last Christmas, from Denmark Vesey, who called at my shop, and informed me of it. Vesey said he was satisfied with his own condition, being free, but as all his children were slaves, he wished to see what could be done for them. He asked me to join, but I then positively refused to do so. I inquired of him, how many he had enlisted, and he mentioned the names of Peter Poyas, Ned Bennett, Rolla Bennett, and Jack Purcell. I inquired if those were all and he replied "yes." He then departed, and had no further correspondence with me until about three months ago. I was then walking in Wentworth Street on my way to a man named Peet Smith, up King Street, and was accosted by Frank Ferguson, who told me, he had just returned from the country, and had *collected four plantations of Negroes.* He requested me to inform Vesey, that he would call on him that evening, and give him an account of his *operations in the country.* I went to Jack Purcell and requested him to carry the message for me, as I was busy. On my return home in the evening, I met Vesey's son-in-law at my door, who said that Vesey wished to see me. I accompanied him to Vesey's, and there found Peter Poyas, Ned Bennett, Gullah Jack, Frank, and his fellow servant, Adam Ferguson. Frank then informed Vesey, he had collected four plantations of Negroes, and said he would start on Saturday the 15th of June, to bring them to town, on the 16th. He said, he would conduct them into the woods, and place them, about three miles from town, until Sunday night. Vesey then again urged me to join, and I consented. This was about three months prior to the 16th of June. Vesey, from that time, continued to visit the shop in which I worked. Peter, Ned, Vesey, Frank, Rolla, Adam, Gullah Jack, Jack Purcell, and myself were the party at Vesey's, and there agreed to enlist as many men as we could. Vesey *even ceased working himself at his trade, and employed himself exclusively in enlisting men,* and continued to do so until he was apprehended. Shortly afterwards Vesey said he would endeavor to open a correspondence with Port-au-Prince, in Santo Domingo, to ascertain

whether the inhabitants there would assist us. He said he would
send letters there and I advised him to do so, if he could. Sometime after this he brought a letter to me, which was directed to
President Boyer, and was enclosed in a cover, which was directed
to the uncle of the cook of the vessel by which it was sent. The
name of this cook was William. His uncle was to open the en-
velope, and present the letter to Boyer. This vessel, a schooner,
had been repaired at the shipyard, at Gadsden's Wharf, and was
afterwards brought to Vanderhorst's Wharf, where she was then
lying. I walked with Vesey to the wharf—Peirault was in company
with us, at the time. Vesey asked William the cook, if he would
carry the letter for him, and he consented to do so. We then returned, each of us to his respective home—nothing extraordinary
took place after this, and I met no other band or association after
this time, but Vesey's particular company. *Bacchus Hammet
brought a keg of powder to my shop, and said he would procure
five hundred* (500) *muskets from his master's store on the night
of the 16th June.* Bacchus also told me, that he could procure
more powder, but did not say where. The plan was to break
open all the stores where arms were deposited, and seize them,
after they had procured the five hundred muskets above-mentioned.
Vesey said he would appoint his leaders, and places of meeting,
about one week before the 16th of June, but the meeting for this
purpose was prevented by the capture of some of the principals
before that period. Vesey determined to kill both women and
children, but I opposed him and offended him in doing so. Peter
and the rest agreed to the opinion of Vesey in the murder of all.
Sometime before any discoveries or apprehensions were made,
myself and Peirault wished to drop the business, but thought we
had gone too far to retreat. I knew personally of no arms, except
six pikes, shown to me by Gullah Jack, which were made by
Tom Russel. I knew of no lists except the one which I kept,
containing about forty names, and which I destroyed after the
first interruption and alarm. It was said that William Paul had a
list, but I never saw it. William Garner told me that he was to
command the draymen, and that he had procured twelve or thirteen
horses. Jack Purcell told me that *Scipio Simms had been at the
Savannah's, in the neighborhood of Bacon's Bridge, to obtain men.*

Denbo Martin belonged to the party, and informed me that Stephen Smith acknowledged that he was one.

Charles Drayton and Peirault have both seen Denbo at my shop. *Vesey originally proposed the second Sunday, or the 14th of July, as the day for rising,* but afterwards changed it to the 16th of June. After the plot was discovered, Vesey said it was all over unless an attempt was made to *rescue those who might be condemned,* by rushing on the people and saving the prisoners, or all dying together. Vesey said, that as Peter and Ned were accustomed to go into the country they must go there and recruit men. Vesey was in the habit of going to Bulkley's Farm—*William Palmer and Vesey were very intimate.* Jack Purcell knew of this conspiracy before myself—I do not recollect any person who refused when I applied to him. Some took time to consider, but they all finally agreed. Vesey was considered by the whole party, as a man of great capacity, and was also thought to possess a bloody disposition. He had, I am told, in the course of his life, seven wives, and had travelled through almost every part of the world, with his former master Captain Vesey, and spoke French with fluency. Morris Brown, Harry Drayton, and Charles Corr, and other influential leaders of the African Church, were never consulted on this subject, for fear they would betray us to the whites. Vesey had many years ago a pamphlet on the slave trade. Vesey said that his eldest stepson was engaged in this affair.

The Court had, previously to this confession, twice applied for and obtained from the Governor a respite for Monday, Charles Drayton, and Harry Haig, with a view to obtain from them the testimony and information they appeared willing to give. On the 24th day of July, after Monday had made his last confession, they addressed the following letter to the Governor.

Charleston, 24th July, 1822.

Sir,

We recommend that Monday Gell, Charles Drayton, and Harry Haig should be pardoned upon condition that they be sent out of the limits of the United States. We feel it our duty to state to your Excellency the reasons which have influenced us in this measure. These men are unquestionably guilty of the

offences with which they have been charged; but under the
impression that they would ultimately have their lives spared,
they have made to us disclosures not only important in the
detection of the general plan of the conspiracy, but enabling
the Court to convict a number of the principal offenders. Having used these individuals as witnesses and obtained from
them the knowledge they could communicate, we deemed it
unnecessarily harsh and amounting almost to treachery, afterwards to sacrifice their lives. In addition to this inducement,
we regard it to be politic that the Negroes should know that
even their principal advisers and ringleaders cannot be confided in, and that under the temptation of exemption from
capital punishment they will betray the common cause.

On the next day they received an answer, in which the Governor declines pardoning conditionally, Monday, Charles, and
Harry, and says, "the cases of Monday Gell, Charles Drayton,
and Harry Haig, would produce me considerable embarrassment,
were you not clothed with authority to carry your recommenda-
tion into full effect."

THE COURT then resolved to reconsider the sentence they had
passed on Monday, Charles, and Harry, unanimously altered their
sentence, and passed upon them the following: "That they be
imprisoned in the Work House of Charleston, until their masters,
under the direction of the City Council of Charleston, shall send
them out of the limits of the United States, into which they are
not to return under penalty of death."

THE TRIAL OF CHARLES, a Negro man, belonging to the
Honorable John Drayton—his owner attending.

Evidence

EDWIN, Mr. Paul's slave—For his testimony see page 65.

PATRICK, a Negro man belonging to Miss Datty, testified as
follows: I know Charles Drayton, who asked me in the streets
about five months ago if I would join with him. I asked him what
—he said we want to make up a company. I asked for what—he
said for some respectable brown man coming here from abroad—
I said I did not want death to take me yet.

WITNESS NO. 10, gave the following testimony: I met Charles Drayton before the 16th June at Monday Gell's shop; I was going to market and Charles called to me. I afterwards met him on 1st July in the streets, when he said now get ready, we must break out at once, for we will not let six lives be taken. I asked him where they would begin. He said at Boundary Street directly as the Patrol and Light-Horse turned in. I said had you not better wait 'til after the 4th July—he said no, because in the mean time the people will be hanged. Charles said they had force enough and we parted. I met him in market, 'twixt eight and nine o'clock on 2d July and said to him, now the people are hanged I suppose you are sorry you joined in the business. He said yes and we parted. Monday and Charles were very much together. On Monday, 1st July, Charles Drayton told me that there would be an insurrection on the *morning of the 6th July as soon as the guard turned in—he said he commanded the country born company.* Charles Drayton said he had prepared for himself a gun and a sword.

GEORGE, a Negro man belonging to Mr. Vanderhorst, testified as follows: Gullah Jack is an enemy of the white people. Charles Drayton told me that he would die with Gullah Jack, this was about the time of the execution. I was in the company of Witness No. 10, who asked me to join, and carried me to Jack's house, where they met, and which is next to Monday Gell's—he said he was ready to join, and asked me to join. There I met Gullah Jack, Witness No. 10, John Horry, Harry Haig, Julius Forrest, and Charles Drayton, and others whose names I don't recollect or know—this was after the 16th June—there it was said they would come against the white people. (Jesse's confession[18] see latter part of it, page 58.)

THE COURT unanimously found Charles guilty, and passed upon him the sentence of death.

Subsequently to his conviction he made the following confession: I have seen Peirault Strohecker talking with Monday Gell in his shop. Jack Purcell said to me just before I was taken up, that he had gone into the country to gather the people's mind on this subject, but the overseer was so watchful that he had no chance of speaking to the people.

I heard William Palmer say in Monday Gell's shop, that he was one. I met Pharo Thompson at Monday Gell's—he said what he would do when they commenced—that he had no sword, but that he had a part of a saw which he would have ground into a sword—that he was one. He bragged of what he would do with his sword. Mingo Harth came once to Monday Gell's when I was there, and he then spoke to the effect that he was one of them, but I can't recollect his words—his brother also told me that Mingo had joined. Lewis the mattress maker said to me one day that he had something particular to say to me, of what was going to happen here, but that as he was a country born they did not choose him—I took his meaning.

Lewis Remoussin told me one day, that when it broke out he would be one, and in the mean time he would be leagued in it—this was before the 16th of June.

Sandy Vesey said he knew as much about this business as anyone, and was engaged in it—this was after Jesse was taken up.

Miss Datty's cook, a Frenchman, said to me, as I was a country born, I should not know anything of what was going on 'til the horn blew and it broke out.

I heard Tom Russel say in Monday Gell's shop that he was to make the pikes—Monday at the same time was working, and may or may not have heard him.

The same reasons which induced the Court to alter Monday's sentence to transportation, induced them to alter Charles' to the same.

THE TRIAL OF JOHN, a Negro man, the property of Elias Horry—his owner attending.

Evidence

WITNESS NO. 10, testified as follows: John, Mr. Elias Horry's coachman, came to me one day and asked me what I thought; everyone is ready said John to fight the whites—are you ready? He said "I am ready." This took place sometime before the 16th of June, and every day he asked me the same questions. He came to me very often, and once said he had a sword, and that as soon as it broke out he would go upstairs and kill his master and family. On the 17th of June, on his carriage box he expressed himself to me in the same manner that he had done previous to the 16th.

GEORGE, Mr. Vanderhorst's Negro man slave gave the following evidence: John Horry and myself have conversed on this subject—he said he would be ready with these men whenever they were ready, and spoke much against the whites, saying that he would slaughter them and what he would do. I have met John Horry with others at the meetings at Gullah Jack's.

THE COURT unanimously found John guilty, and passed upon him the sentence of death.

THE TRIAL OF GULLAH JACK, a Negro man, belonging to Mr. Pritchard—his owner attending.

Evidence

WITNESS NO. 10, testified as follows: Jack Pritchard also called on me about this business—he is sometimes called Gullah Jack, sometimes Cooter Jack. He gave me some dry food, consisting of parched corn and ground nuts, and said eat that and nothing else on the morning it breaks out, and when you join us as we pass put into your mouth this crab-claw and you can't then be wounded, and said he, I give the same to the rest of my troops—if you drop the large crab-claw out of your mouth, then put in the small one. Said I, when do you break out and have you got arms—he said a plenty, but they are over Boundary Street, we can't get at them now, but as soon as the Patrol was slack they could get them. This was previous to the 16th June, on which day he said they were to break out. On that day he came to me and said they would not break out that night as the Patrol was too strong—he said he would let me know when they were ready. That Sunday fortnight, the 30th June, he came to me and said I must lay by, they would not break out then, that he had been round to all his company and found them cowards. I said thank God then—he said give me back my corn and cullah (that is crab-claw) I said I would not and upbraided him for having deluded so many. He said all his countryborn promised to join because he was a doctor (that is a conjurer). He said the white people were looking for him and he was afraid of being taken; that two men came to his master's wharf and asked him if he knew Gullah Jack, and that he told them no—*he said his charms would not protect him from the treachery of his own color.* He went away and I have not seen him since. On the 16th June, Jack requested me to let twelve men sleep at my wife's, as they were to break out that night and he wanted them to be near Boundary Street, near to King Street where my wife lives—on being refused he departed in anger and reproached me. George Vanderhorst called on me yesterday morning and asked if I knew that Charles Drayton was taken up, and said he was afraid Charles would name him, not because he was on his list, for he had joined Jack's Company, but because Charles had met him at Gullah Jack's when they were consulting on the subject—that if he heard that Charles had named him he would run off. On Monday, 1st July, Charles Drayton told me that there would be an insurrection on the *morning of the 6th July, as soon as the Guards turned in—he said he commanded the country born company.* Jack told me on the 1st July the same thing, and in addition that they were to rush with their dirks, guns, and swords they had got, kill the City Guard, and take all the arms in the Arsenal—he also said there were some arms in King Street beyond Boundary Street, in the possession of a white man which they intended to take (alluding to the arms of the Charleston Neck Company, deposited at Mr. Wharton's in King Street).

The blacks would have risen on the night of the 16th June, had the Guards not been so strong. This I know from Gullah Jack and Harry Haig, who said, that if the Guards were not too strong they would get the arms near the lines, but if the Guards were out, they could not get them to break out with—("Jack is a little man, a Gullah Negro, with small hands and feet and large whiskers, and belongs to Mr. Pritchard," was the description given of him by this witness, and by which Jack was apprehended.)

Gullah Jack when apprehended denied to the Court that he ever wore whiskers, although the map of a large pair of them was plainly discernible on his face, and continued to deny it stoutly until confronted with his owner—he also positively denied that he ever pretended to be a doctor or conjurer.

Mr. Paul Pritchard deposed as follows: My slave Jack always

wore a very large pair of whiskers which he prized very much, and which nothing could induce him to cut off, and which I often threatened to shave off as a punishment when he misbehaved. These whiskers I found he had cut off to my great surprise about three days ago, and wondered at the cause of it, little dreaming that it was to prevent his being apprehended by a description of him. I did hear some years ago that Jack was a doctor or conjurer —he is called Gullah Jack and Cooter Jack.

GEORGE, Mr. Vanderhorst's slave, gave the testimony following: Gullah Jack is an enemy of the white people. I attended a meeting of several at his house, and he was the head man there. All present agreed to join & come against the whites. Jack was my leader—he is the head of the Gullah Company. I heard that among them they had charms. Jack said if any man betrayed them, they would injure him, and I was afraid to inform. The little man standing before me is Gullah Jack, who had large black whiskers, which he has cut since I saw him last. If I am accepted as a witness and my life spared, I must beg the Court to send me away from this place, *as I consider my life in great danger from having given testimony.* I have heard it said all about the streets, generally, I can't name anyone in particular, that whoever is the white man's friend, God help them; from which I understood they would be killed—I was afraid of Gullah Jack as a conjurer.[19]

WILLIAM, Mr. Paul's slave, gave the following evidence: Mingo Harth told me that he knows the little man who can't be shot, who told him that there was a Gullah Society going on which met once a month.

WITNESS NO. 5, testified that "the little man who can't be killed, shot or taken, is" named Jack, a Gullah Negro.

FRANK, Mrs. Ferguson's slave testified as follows: The first time I spoke with Monday Gell was one night at Denmark Vesey's house, where I heard Vesey tell Monday that he must *send one into the country to bring the people down.* Monday said *he had sent up Jack* and told him *to tell the people to come down and join in the fight* against the whites, and also to ascertain and inform him how many people he could get. A few days after, I met Vesey, Monday, and Jack in the street, under Mr. Duncan's trees, at night, where *Jack stated he had been into the country round by Goose Creek and Dorchester,* and that he had spoken to 6,600 persons who had agreed to join.

THE COURT unanimously found Gullah Jack guilty, and passed upon him the sentence of death.

Subsequently to his conviction, Harry Haig, who received sentence of death at the same time that he did, made the following confession:

"Julius Forrest and myself always worked together. Gullah Jack calls himself a Doctor Negro—he induced Julius and myself to join at last, but at first we refused. Before the 16th of June, Jack appointed to meet us at Bulkley's farm—when we got there Jack was not there, but Peter Poyas came—we broke up at day light. Not quite a month before the 16th of June, Jack met us and talked about war—I asked Jack what he would do for arms —bye and bye, said Jack, we will have arms—he said he would have some arms made at the blacksmith's. Jack was going to give me[20] . . . I refused to do this as I considered it murder, and that God would never pardon me for it; it was not like fair fighting. Until Jack was taken up and condemned to death, I felt as if I was bound up, and had not the power to speak one word about it. Jack charmed Julius and myself at last, and we then consented to join. Tom Russel the blacksmith and Jack are partners (in conjuring), Jack taught him to be a doctor. Tom talked to Jack about the fighting and agreed to join, and those two brought Julius and myself to agree to it. Jack said Tom was his second and "when you don't see me, and see Tom, you see me." Jack said Tom was making arms for the black people—Jack said he could not be killed, nor could a white man take him."

THE TRIAL OF HARRY, a Negro man belonging to Mr. David Haig—James Haig, Esq., attending as counsel for his owner.

Evidence

WITNESS NO. 10, testified as follows: After Peter Poyas had twice called on me about this business, he and Harry Haig called on me. I was not at home, but the next morning I met Harry who asked me for my name—I refused it—he said I would be killed if I did not join. I said I would join when they came out, if they were stronger than the whites. Harry called on me again, and asked me if I was willing, that the thing would break out soon. I asked him where he would begin—he said in Boundary Street—at what hour—he said at twelve o'clock at night or early in the morning as soon as the Guard were discharged. Harry Haig has since seen me several times, and told me to hold myself ready. I said I'm ready when called on. He said all the draymen came to his master's cooper-yard, and said they were ready, but he told them he was waiting for Gullah Jack. He said he would tell me when they were ready, that they were only waiting for the head man, who was a white man; but he, although asked, would neither tell me the white man's name, nor where the powder and arms were. This was last Tuesday, the very day six Negroes were hanged, about 6 A.M. This was the last time we spoke though I have seen him since.

GEORGE, Mr. Vanderhorst's slave gave the evidence which follows: I have met Harry Haig at Gullah Jack's, where he and all agreed to join and come against the whites. I can't say *he* was afraid of Gullah Jack as a conjurer—I was—I have often seen Harry with Julius Forrest.

THE COURT unanimously found Harry guilty, and passed upon him the sentence of death. (After his conviction, he confessed his guilt—see page 79.)

The reasons which induced the Court to alter the sentences passed on Monday and Charles to transportation, induced them to alter Harry's to the same.

THE TRIAL OF JULIUS, a Negro man belonging to Mr. T. H. Forrest—his owner attending.

Evidence

PRUDENCE, a Negro woman, the property of Mr. Bussacre, testified as follows: The first time I conversed with Julius Forrest on this business was previous to the execution of the six Negroes—'twas a Sunday night about a fortnight ago, that he called at my house and said he had just come from the Island—that he had been looking for Harry Haig but could not find him. He said that he and Harry were to have gone up the road on Sunday the 16th

June to meet the black people who were coming to fight in town, but that the white people having got wind of it and turned out too strong, they were obliged to go away. He came again last Sunday night to my house and said Harry Haig was taken up for the same thing he had been talking to me about that Sunday night, and asked me if I had said anything to any person about what he had said, as they have taken up Harry Haig. He said, I suppose my time will come next, but if Harry doesn't call my name I shall be safe—this was our last conversation.

MR. T. H. FORREST deposed that Prudence is like a kind of mother to Julius, having raised or brought him up. Harry Haig and Julius are very intimate and are together at her shop almost every night.

GEORGE, Mr. Vanderhorst's slave testified as follows: I met Julius at Gullah Jack's meeting, where he, together with all, agreed to join and come against the white people. The man now standing before me is Julius Forrest, whom I have often seen with Harry Haig. (Harry Haig's confession, see on page 79.)

THE COURT unanimously found Julius guilty, and passed upon him the sentence of death.[21]

THE TRIAL OF TOM, a Negro man, the slave of Mrs. Russel— James Gray, Esq., attending for his owner.

Evidence

PEIRAULT,[22] a Negro man belonging to Mr. J. Strohecker, testified as follows: Tom told me at his shop that he had joined Gullah Jack's band—I know he belongs to this band—I belong to Monday Gell's. These bands were to rise against the whites, and Tom told me himself that he would rise with the band against the whites. I saw six pike heads at Monday Gell's shop, three of them were like spears, and three like bayonets, with holes in them to fix in poles. I met Tom at Vesey's house, where it was agreed that the 16th June should be the day for the rising, and there also was Gullah Jack. Monday had a list with forty-two names on it, mine was one—he burned his list when Peter Poyas was taken up.

Cross-examined by Mr. Gray, the prisoner's counsel—The

first time I met Tom at Vesey's was on the 16th June—when I went to Vesey's I met him there. I knew him long before. Tom was willing to agree to all that was adopted there, but did not talk himself. I met Charles Drayton at Tom's shop. Smart Anderson was present when the spears were brought into Monday's shop.

Re-examined—I saw Gullah Jack carry those spears to Monday Gell's.

CHARLES gave the following evidence: Tom told me himself in Monday's shop that he was making the pikes for Gullah Jack.

Cross-examined—I did not meet Peirault at Tom's shop, but at Monday's—I never was in company with Tom and Peirault together on this business.

MONDAY testified as follows: Tom and Charles Drayton talked together in my shop once, but I did not hear what they said—I had frequent conversations with Peirault, but not with Tom.

MRS. MARK MARKS deposed as follows: Mrs. Russel the prisoner's owner told me that Gullah Jack was constantly with Tom at breakfast, dinner, and supper, and that she cautioned Tom not to have so much to do with Jack or he would be taken up.

[*Note*. Mr. Gray consented to this testimony being received instead of sending for Mrs. Russel.]

JAMES MALL, a white lad, about 16 or 17 years of age, a witness on behalf of the prisoner, deposed as follows: I was working with Tom in his shop from February to last of March. I then went into the country and received a message from him sometime after to come down and work in his shop with him again. I came down about the last of May and he refused to employ me. One day when I went to his shop I saw him making something like a knife a foot long, out of a file which he had not yet finished—he makes edged tools.

Cross-examined by the Court—When I was working with Tom I did not eat any meals at the shop but at home. Gullah Jack was frequently at Tom's shop, and they frequently talked together in Gullah, which I do not understand. Tom said, after the people were taken up, that he would not do as some had done, tell upon one another for money.

THE COURT unanimously found Tom guilty, and passed upon him the sentence of death.

THE TRIAL OF LOUIS REMOUSSIN, a Negro man, the slave of Mr. Cromwell—his owner attending.

Evidence

PEIRAULT testified as follows: I know Louis—Louis and Joe and myself met in the street, and Joe said to me Louis was one to join against the whites; Louis did not deny it, this was on the 15th of June. Louis said he was ready to rise against the white people. Joe said the French Band had been ready a long time. This is all I know against Louis—the conversation was in Creole French, I understand it. (*The Court required Louis and Peirault to speak together in French, which they did, and Peirault evidently understood that language.*)

CHARLES testified as follows: Louis met me one day as he came out of the Work House. He one day said to me that he had not much to do with the business, but that on the night the attack commenced against the whites, he would be ready, and he told me to get ready—I understood from his conversation plainly enough that he was one of them.

Cross-examined—This was the Saturday before the thing was to break out. I met him at his own house—he told me at Monday Gell's, to come to his house to talk about this business. I have seen him often at Monday's.

MONDAY gave the following evidence: Louis came to my shop and told me to go to his house that night, that he wanted to see me about something particular—I did not go though.

THE COURT unanimously found Louis Remoussin guilty, and passed upon him the sentence of death, but recommended to the Governor to pardon him upon condition that he be transported out of the limits of the United States.

THE TRIAL OF JOE, a Negro man belonging to Mr. Jore— his owner attending.

Evidence

PEIRAULT testified as follows: I met Joe at the corner of Boundary and Wall Streets; he said to me how does this business stand now—this affair—he said I don't want to go home before

I see how this business, meaning the rising against the whites, terminates. He was then a runaway and belonged to the man who keeps a shoe shop in King Street, by Mr. Hart's. We parted, the next time we met it was at Monday Gell's, when the spears were on the table. Joe said to Monday Gell in my presence that the French people would be ready when they were ready, and that he was one of them. The third time I met Joe was when we met Louis. After Louis parted, Joe said that his master's store in King Street was not yet open, and that there were plenty of arms at Mr. Duquercron's store, near the Inspection, even to bayonets— he said that when we raised, we must all run in there, break the door open and get arms.

Cross-examined by Mr. Jore—He told me that he had run-away, but I don't know it myself—this was about the 1st June. The second time was before anyone was taken up on this business. The third time I met him was on 15th June—our meetings were accidental.

CHARLES gave the evidence following: I met Joe three or four times at Monday's—he generally speaks as in a parable—that is, gives hints. He said the French Band was armed throughout, and were ready, and he was ready; but he did not know how to trust countryborns; this he said in Monday's presence.

MONDAY testified as follows: Joe has often been at my shop, and he and I talked of this concern—he said he knew the French who were to join, but as they did not speak to him he did not speak to them—that he was one of those who had joined. This was better than a month ago.

Cross-examined by Mr. Jore—He comes to my shop as a friend to get me to do work for him—he insinuated that he would be an active man.

MR. JORE AND COL. CROSS testified that Joe's general conduct was good.

THE COURT unanimously found Joe guilty, and passed upon him the sentence of death.

THE TRIAL OF MINGO, a Negro man, the property of Mr. William Harth—his owner attending.

Evidence

MONDAY testified as follows: Mingo told me in my shop that Peter Poyas had told him of this business, and that he was to take his master's horse and act as a horseman in the fight.

Cross-examined by Mr. Harth—This was before Peter was taken up on the 2d June—he was often at my shop, and knows me well. He asked me if I knew Peter—I said yes, and that he had spoken to me, he said he had spoken to him too. I sometimes visit the society he belongs to—George Wilson is his class leader.

CHARLES gave the following testimony: I have seen Mingo Harth at Monday Gell's—he was talking about the rising—he said expressly he was one.

Cross-examined by Mr. Harth—This was after William and Edwin were taken up.

WILLIAM, a Negro man belonging to Mr. John Paul testified as follows: I have heard something about an insurrection of the blacks, but was not concerned in it. Mr. William Harth's Negro man Mingo told me about it, and referred me to Peter Poyas for further information, who he said had a list with 9,000 names upon it, and that he was still taking down names. On the week I was to see Peter I was apprehended. Mingo said that 6,000 men on the Bay were already down on the list in Peter's possession. Mingo would not own before the wardens what he told me. I never had any conversation with Peter. Mingo said his name was not yet down, and he would not put it down 'til he knew all that was to be done—that Ned Bennett knew all about it, and told it to all Mr. Bennett's people, and that letters were passing between those concerned. I can read and count printed characters but not written. On a Saturday night Mingo told me as we were going towards his wife's house, that every day at two o'clock Peter went to Mr. Harth's lumber yard and talked to the other men about this matter, to make them sensible of the plan. At Mingo's house I took up the Bible and read two chapters from the prophet Tobit—Mingo said that *all those belonging to the African Church are engaged in the insurrection, from the country to the town—that there is a little man among them who can't be shot, killed, or caught, who was to be their general, and who would provide them with arms—that some arms were provided but he did not tell me where they were,* and he also said that Ned Bennett and Charles Shubrick are officers. Peter, Ned, and Charles I know to be class leaders in the African Church. The African Association has also a Church in Anson Street near Boundary Street, and one in Cow Alley, where they have services. I believe that Mingo was endeavoring to get me to join them in the rising, and from his conversation I have no doubt but that he was engaged in the conspiracy, and that all he said to me was to get me to join them. *It was also told to me that our color from the North to the South had combined together to fight against New Orleans.* Mingo was no doubt satisfied that I would join. I never had any conversation with anyone about the rising but with Mingo and Col. Prioleau's man. Mingo said that Peter Poyas would tell me when the rising would take place—that Mr. Bennett's Ned was one of them—*that Denmark Vesey was the chief man and more concerned than anyone else.* I beg you won't take up Sarah, for no woman knows anything about it. Mingo said that letters were passing between Peter Poyas, Ned Bennett, and Charles Shubrick. I am persuaded that Denmark Vesey was chiefly concerned in this business. Mingo said that the country places were engaged in the plot, and also the Islands—that he knows the little man who can't be shot, who told him that there was a *Gullah Society* going on which met once a month—that all the orders he got were from Peter. Mingo always denied that he was engaged, and yet always talked to me as if he wanted me to join. Mingo said they would get horses, which were engaged at one, two, or three livery stables from the stable boys; two stables he named in particular, viz: Mr. Billings' and the one behind the old Church. Mingo said a brown man, the steward of the cutter, had stolen some of the arms, and that Jim, a blacksmith of Mr. Bennett made arms.

GEORGE, a Negro man belonging to Mr. Wilson, a witness on behalf of the prisoner, testified as follows: I never saw Monday Gell at my Society—he would not have been admitted, as he was a member of the African Association. Cross-examined—He might have been there and I not have known it, as there are sometimes 60 or 100 persons present.

PETER PARLER, a free black man, a witness on behalf of the

prisoner, testified as follows: I have never seen Monday Gell at my Society. Cross-examined—I am generally at the meetings unless I am sick.

THE COURT unanimously found Mingo guilty, and passed upon him the sentence of death.

THE TRIAL OF JACK, a mulatto man, belonging to Mrs. Purcell —Mr. Thomas Smith, the brother of his owner, attending.

Evidence

MONDAY testified as follows: I have seen Jack and Vesey talking together before my door—he told me that he was one of those to rise against the whites, and Vesey told me so before. The message that Frank Ferguson gave to me to give to Vesey, I got Jack to carry to Vesey for me. The message was, that he had just come from the country, that he had there got four plantations of men to join—and to go to Vesey and ask him to be at home tonight, as he would call on him. I know he carried it, because Vesey told me so that night. He came to my shop afterwards and said to me he was looking for Vesey, and be sure that I called no name.

FRANK testified as follows: I know Jack Purcell, but don't know that he is concerned in this business. I did give to Monday Gell a message for Vesey.

CHARLES gave the following evidence: Jack told me he had been at his Mistress' Plantation and tried to get the people to join in this business—but could not go again. He said he had joined, and asked me where Lot Forrester lived, that he was the proper person to go into the country to bring the people down.

THE PRISONER asked permission to cross-examine Charles, which was granted; but his questions were such, that no one could well answer them but himself. In the course of this examination he admitted, that a large meeting had been called on Stono by Lot, and that considerable preparations were made to receive him, but that Lot did not attend, and he was requested to reprove him for not doing so.

THE COURT unanimously found Jack guilty, and passed upon him the sentence of death. A few moments preceding his execution, he made the following confession to the Intendant of Charleston:

If it had not been for the cunning of that old villain Vesey, I should not now be in my present situation. He employed every stratagem to induce me to join him. He was in the habit of reading to me all the passages in the newspapers that related to Santo Domingo, and apparently every pamphlet he could lay his hands on, that had any connection with slavery. He one day brought me a speech which he told me had been delivered in Congress by a Mr. King on the subject of slavery; he told me this Mr. King was the black man's friend, that Mr. King had declared he would continue to speak, write, and publish pamphlets against slavery as long as he lived, until the Southern States consented to emancipate their slaves, for that slavery was a disgrace to the country.

THE TRIAL OF SMART, a Negro man, the slave of Mr. Robert Anderson—his owner and M. King, Esq., his counsel attending.

Evidence

FRANK testified as follows: I have seen the prisoner at Vesey's— he told me in the presence of Vesey he had joined and would be ready whenever called on. Vesey sent him one evening to call me.

Cross-examined by Mr. King—I think at Vesey's there were then present, Monday and Charles and others.

MONDAY gave the following evidence: I saw Smart at Vesey's in the day—Peirault and Peter Cooper were also there. I have often conversed with him on this business, and he seemed to be as much in it as possible. I never asked this man to join. Vesey brought all of us into it. He belongs to the same gang that I did.

Cross-examined by Mr. King—I was not the first man who spoke to him. I first saw him at Vesey's—he was very much attached to me and called me Pa, and my wife Ma. I don't know that he ever got anyone to join, and think he would have told me if he had—he was just such another as myself. I had a list with about forty on it, *but tore it up on the first discovery.* He belongs to the African Church.

PEIRAULT gave the testimony following: Smart is a drayman, and engaged in this business and in the same company, and confessed the same to me. I have met him at Vesey's and at Bulkley's Farm. I met him at Vesey's on Sunday in the day, and Monday

Gell was also there, where we talked about the rising. The second time I met him at Bulkley's Farm there were thirteen in all—Smart and I have often spoken and promised to fight by one another against the white people. On Saturday the 15th June, Smart got two *muskets from Mr. Fordham's shop to carry up to Gadsden's Wharf,* they were shortly after taken away from Smart's dray, on which he was carrying them—and he made off by himself. I was present, *one was for me, one for Smart*—we borrowed the muskets from my brother.

Cross-examined by Mr. King—I met him twice at Vesey's—Smart told me first and got me to join.

THE COURT unanimously found Smart guilty, and passed upon him the sentence of death.

When Smart was arraigned he pleaded guilty to the charge, and his counsel handed to the Court his confession in writing; but the Court advising that the plea of guilty should be withdrawn, his counsel did so and pleaded not guilty. The confession handed to the Court was not used against him, but is now given to the public.

"Monday Gell invited me to go up the road to Mr. Bulkley's Farm, on Sunday about three months ago, where there were upwards of thirty persons present, and among them Bulkley's man Billy—I said I would not trust countrymen. I believe Denmark Vesey was there, but did not see him. About four months ago, or going on four months, William Garner, drayman, told me he expected people from Santo Domingo; white people would kill as many as they could. I call Monday Gell, Pa, and his wife, Ma. About three weeks before going up to the farm, Monday Gell asked me to join him, by telling me that they were in servitude, kicked and cuffed and abused. He spoke to me about Santo Domingo—people turn and fight the white people. I said we can't do that, but Gell said we could make a contrivance to do it. Monday Gell told me that Gullah wanted to begin when the Negroes of the African Church were taken up in 1818—that if I told anything they would kill me, and made me hold up my hand and swear not to tell anything.

I asked when they intended to rise, he said on Saturday night previous to death of Dr. M'Call. Monday told me the old man said we must begin tonight about ten o'clock. I said to Monday, he must stop it, that Monday must send word to the old man to stop it, that it was a great sin.

I met with Monday Gell a black man named Jack Glen, a painter.

When at the farm of Mr. Bulkley, we meet a snake at the gate, which the old man Vesey killed, and one of them says, that's the way we would do it. I seen Monday, and he says, they had better begin about eight o'clock, before the Guard meet, and if they don't do that, meet away on the Green, somewhere by the lines, march down through the streets, come down to the Guard House. Monday told me there were three or four gangs. I asked him some questions about the mode of attack, which I consented to. Monday told me that they would have a meeting, or setting up at night, and begin then.

I did not agree to have a fire in the city. At a meeting at Monday Gell's house, Denmark Vesey present, I asked him if he was going to kill the women and children—Denmark answered, what was the use of killing the louse and leaving the nit. I said my God what a sin—Denmark Vesey told me I had not a man's heart, and that I was a friend to Buckra. Monday Gell told me that they sent to several places in the country.

Jack Glen, a black man, wanted to borrow my horse to go up the country. I said I had not one to lend—he said he must go in the country that day Sunday, to Goose Creek.

The time I was at the farm they told me they had long things like my arm to put handles to, that they would make contrivance.

Vesey told me one day, after they had taken the place, they would take the money, and he would go in a vessel and put as many as he could, and go back to his own country.

Vesey told me that all the powder was about three miles out of town, and they must take it—could easily get it; and they knew about a place in Queen Street, opposite the Planters' Hotel, where there was arms. The old man, Denmark Vesey, said that they were to attack the Guard House, in three or four ways, and then they would get all the arms.

I never heard about sending the two persons to Santo Domingo. Monday told me they were about to engage some draymen in it, but did not know how to trust them.

Monday told me that they meet every other night, and he would tell me more about it, when he saw me again. The old man (meaning Vesey) told me to get some draymen who had horses, and if I was a good rider he would make me a captain of a troop.

When they met they did not pray at the meeting in the kitchen. I was only at the Neck meeting about one hour; Peter Poyas was not at that meeting. I told Monday not to put my name on the list that they had. Peter was not at that meeting, but was to go with us. Monday said he expected Peter there. I have no knowledge of any deposit of arms, ammunition, or powder—I did not promise to any particular act in the business, or know of any other persons engaged in the business than those I have already mentioned—I never asked any person to join.

THE TRIAL OF PHARO, a mulatto man, the property of Mr. John N. Thompson—his owner and David Ramsay, Esq., his counsel attending.

Evidence

CHARLES testified as follows: Pharo told me himself in Monday's shop that he was engaged in the conspiracy. I met him one day with a scythe in his cart, which he told me he was carrying to a blacksmith's to have made into a sword. About a week after, and previous to the 16th June, he said he was going to meet some young men who could tell him all about it—I have met him several times at Monday's.

Cross-examined by Mr. Ramsay—He bragged of what he could and would do with the white people. I did not hear Pharo tell a man to make a candlestick for him.

MONDAY testified as follows: I know from our talk about it together that Pharo was one—he said he was making ready for the rising. Two days after Peter was taken he told me, that if he could get a ticket, and a $50 bill he would take his horse and run away before he would be taken. On Sunday, about two weeks after Peter was taken up the first time (about 19th June) he pointed to the

Archdale Church, where the white people were, and said, when shall we be like them. I said when God pleased. Sunday before I was brought here he carried me to his stable, and said he had told his master he had nothing to do in this business, which was a lie.

Cross-examined by Mr. Ramsay—Charles told me that Pharo had a scythe which he was going to make into a sword.

PEIRAULT gave the following evidence: I know that Pharo is one—one day in the streets we met and conversed on this business, when he told me that he had carried something to a blacksmith to have a sword made for himself. I know he was just as willing as myself to join.

THE COURT unanimously found Pharo guilty, and passed upon him the sentence of death.

THE TRIAL OF SANDY VESEY, a Negro man, the property of J. J. Schnell—his owner attending.

Evidence

CHARLES testified as follows: Sandy had a hand in the rising —he told me that a gentleman had taken him up and asked him if he knew anything about Jesse, that he said no, as there was no occasion to inform—that he knew how to make cartridges, and would make some. He told me in Monday's shop that he was one of those who had joined and was ready.

Cross-examined by Mr. Schnell—He did not tell me to what company he belonged—he never gave his name to be put on a list that I know of.

MONDAY gave the following evidence: Sandy has been in my shop, and he told me he had joined. He said on Sunday the 16th June, in Archdale Street, that he was waiting for Jesse who had gone to get a horse to go into the country. He was frequently in my shop, but only once spoke about this business—he appeared to be anxious and zealous, about it. He belongs to the African Church.

EDWARD P. SIMONS, ESQ., deposed as follows: The day after Jesse was taken up, I examined this fellow, who stated that Jesse had said to him, "Vesey the Guard is too strong tonight." Sandy is a peaceable character—Jesse and himself married sisters.

THE COURT unanimously found Sandy Vesey guilty, and

passed upon him the sentence of death; but recommended to the Governor to pardon him upon condition that he be transported out of the limits of the United States.

THE TRIAL OF PARIS, a Negro man belonging to Miss Ball—Mr. Minot as the friend of his owner attending.

Evidence

MONDAY testified as follows: Paris and Saby Gaillard were frequently in my shop—the week after Peter was taken up he came to me and said, your name is called, be on your guard. He acknowledged he had joined, and frequently came to know how the thing was going on—he belongs to the African Church.

PEIRAULT testified as follows: I know that Paris knew of this business—I saw him at Monday's, and heard him speaking of the business—he was as much in it as I am.

THE COURT unanimously found Paris guilty, and passed upon him the sentence of death, but recommended to the Governor to pardon him upon condition that he be transported out of the limits of the United States.

THE TRIAL OF SABY GAILLARD, a free black man—Mr. Wesner attending on his behalf as his friend.

Evidence

MONDAY testified as follows: Saby frequently came to my shop and talked on this business—he and Denmark Vesey in my shop talked on this business. He took out one day out of his pocket on the Bay, a piece of newspaper, and asked me to read it; I did so at my shop, and afterwards he asked me if I had read it—I said yes—'twas about Boyer's battle in Santo Domingo against the Spaniards, and he said to me afterwards, if he had men he could do the same as Boyer—and that he could whip ten white men himself.

Cross-examined by Mr. Wesner—he agreed with Vesey's discourse, which was to kill the whites.

PEIRAULT gave the evidence following: Saby said to me one day after Peter was taken up "I advise you to have nothing to do with this affair, let the Lord finish it and leave it to those who began it." Monday told me before this that Saby was concerned, and had given him a piece of paper to read.

THE COURT found Saby Gaillard guilty, and passed upon him the sentence of death, but recommended to the Governor to pardon him upon condition that he be transported out of the limits of the United States.

THE TRIAL OF WILLIAM, a Negro man, the slave of Mrs. Colcock—Mr. D. D. Bacot attending as the friend of his owner.

Evidence

MONDAY testified as follows: William has often been at my shop and asked me what was going on——I did not tell him anything. One day he said to me a brother told him, five hundred men were making up for this purpose——he did not say that he was one.

CHARLES' evidence was as follows: I met William two or three times at Monday's, but did not hear him say he had joined.

PEIRAULT gave this testimony: I met William several times at Monday's, but don't know that he joined.

THE PRISONER in explanation of being so often at Monday's, stated to the Court, "when I went to Monday's it was to hear what was going on in Congress, as we expected that Congress was going to set us free, and as what was going on was printed in all the papers, so that black as well as white might read it." The prisoner had previously stated to Captain T. H. Jervey, who attended the trial, and one of whose wenches is the prisoner's wife, "Pompey Bryan told me that Mrs. Bryan's coachman held a commission, or was one of the officers of Denmark Vesey—that some hundred draymen of this city were to act as horsemen." This was about a month ago (early in June). He also told me that Denmark Vesey had ordered them all out so as to strike the first blow on Saturday night the 15th June. I told him then that I would have nothing to do with it and would go quietly to my bed; he said the same and we parted. One of Colonel Cross' wenches about the house, a yellow complexion, with a small boy about four or five years old, told me that Joseph (Joe Jore), the former cook of Colonel Cross, said that Morris Brown (the Bishop of the African Church) swore on the Bible never to divulge the secret, even if they suffered death. Henry Drayton (alias Harry Bull, one of the Bishops or Ministers of the African Church) in crossing the Mall in front of Flinn's Church, told me on a Sunday afternoon "that the whites wanted nothing but a good spanking with the sword." Pompey Haig told me that there were some Frenchmen, blacks, very skillful in making swords and spears, such as they used in Africa—this was about a month ago. He also told me that there were some Frenchmen determined if those men were hanged, to rise and defend them, and that he heard there was a regular army ready in the woods to defend them.

THE COURT unanimously found William not guilty, and discharged him.

THE TRIAL OF POLYDORE, a Negro man, the property of Mrs. Faber—Mr. C. H. Faber, his owner's brother, attending.

Evidence

BILLY, a Negro man belonging to Mr. Bulkley, testified as follows: Polydore met once at my master's farm, at which meeting Gullah Jack was present—he agreed with the rest to join and raise against the whites. One Sunday early in the morning, when the people were to rise, Polydore brought to the farm those pike poles (pointing to the bundle of pike poles found concealed on the farm and then in court) and told me to let them stay there, that Robert was coming. Polydore belongs to the African Congregation.

HARRY, Mr. Haig's slave, gave the following evidence: Polydore was in Jack's company—I met him at the meeting at Bulkley's Farm, where they were talking about rising against the whites, and Polydore agreed to join in it.

Cross-examined by Mr. Faber—Jack was there, and when he made the proposition to join and raise against the whites, all present gave him an answer to join.

THE COURT unanimously found Polydore guilty, and passed upon him the sentence of death.

THE TRIAL OF ROBERT, a Negro man, the property of John Robertson—his owner attending.

Evidence

CHARLES testified as follows: I met Robert at Tom Russel's, where he went for the pikes, and Tom said to him, the pikes are at your house. Tom Russel asked him if he was not to go into the country for the people—he said he had sent word.

Cross-examined by Mr. Robertson—I saw him at Tom's about dark—it seemed to me from the conversation that he was going to fix on the pikes to the poles.

BILLY's testimony was: Robert belongs to Gullah Jack's Company—he was at the meeting of Gullah Jack's party at Bulkley's Farm. He was at two meetings, and he tried to fire the pistol off but could not. The same day the pike poles were brought he told me not to stir, that the white people had heard of this business. Robert told me that Gullah Jack was the head man in this business —he said Gullah Jack went to Father Morris Brown about this business, and that Father Morris said, I am going to the North, but if you can get men you can try this business, but don't call my name. Anything that Jack wanted he sent Robert for—if anything happened to Jack, Robert would be the next man. When Polydore brought the poles, he said Robert would know what to do with the poles, and when Robert came he said, let the poles lay there, the whites have found out the business.

Cross-examined by Mr. Robertson—There was no dispute between me and the Ropewalk people.

THE COURT unanimously found Robert guilty, and passed upon him the sentence of death.

THE TRIAL OF JACK, a Negro man belonging to Mr. J. S. Glenn.

Evidence   ❧

CHARLES testified as follows: Jack is engaged in this business —we have spoken together, and he told me he belonged to the horse company. I have met him once at Vesey's at a meeting about this business; Glenn there quoted Scripture to prove he would not be condemned for raising against the whites—he read a chapter out of the Bible. I have often met him at Monday's, where he was talking of this business. I have often conversed with him, when he always said he was one, and would rather be a horseman. He belongs to the African Church.

MONDAY's evidence was: Jack was engaged in it—he and I talked about it, and he was making every preparation as well as myself about it. I once saw him at Vesey's when we were talking of the plans. He said as he had lame feet he would rather be a horseman—Vesey looked on him as one of his followers or men. I met him on the evening of the 15th June in the street with Benjamin Campbell—he said, that Ben belonged to the horse, after they had parted. He said he was preparing to rise on Sunday the 16th June. He was often at my shop—Charles Drayton was sometimes present.

PEIRAULT gave the following evidence: Jack was concerned as much as myself. I met him at Monday's first, when he said he was one, and the third time I met him at Vesey's, where we met purposely on this affair—Ned Bennett and Peter Poyas were there. Jack agreed to go into the country to bring down the people to fight against the whites—before the 16th June he sent his wife to me to say he wanted to get my horse to go into the country. At the meeting at Vesey's, Jack carried about a hat to get money to pay a man to make pikes—I gave 12½ cents—Jack put in the same. The second time I met him at the Battery, he said he was going into the country to bring the blacks down—he said he had joined as a horseman. At the meeting at Vesey's besides Ned and Peter, Monday, Charles, Bacchus, and Smart Anderson were present, and John Enslow and several others whose names I know not.

BACCHUS testified as follows: I saw Jack at Vesey's the first time I met there—he was the man who read the Bible—he passed the hat round that night for the contribution—Monday, Charles, Pharo, and Smart, and others whom I knew not were there.

THE COURT unanimously found Jack guilty, and passed upon him the sentence of death.

[*Note.* On the trial of Charles Billings, it was proved, that Jack Glenn intended to sleep at Mr. Billings' Livery Stables on the night of the 16th June, for the purpose of assisting in saddling the horses for the colored people.]

THE TRIAL OF LOT, a Negro man, the property of Mr. Forrester—his owner attending.

Evidence

MONDAY testified as follows: Lot and I have been talking about
this business, and he said he was one engaged in this insurrection
and was making ready, this was at my shop where he frequently
was, and always talking on this business—he was one of the African Church, but I believe he had been turned out.

FRANK's evidence was: I heard Lot tell Vesey that he had gone
up to Santee, but before he had got there he met some black persons who told him that the driver had heard it, and told the overseer, and that he in consequence had to make his escape.

JACK belonging to Mrs. Purcell, gave the following evidence:
Lot was to have gone up to Stono, to a large meeting where they
made great preparations for him, but he did not come—I was then
up there. I afterwards met him at Monday's and taxed him about
not fulfilling his promise—he said his business prevented him.

Jesse before he acknowledged his guilt, requested that Lot,
who was not at that time suspected, might be sent for and made
to confront him. This being done he first confessed his own guilt,
and then charged Lot with being an accomplice, and said in an
impressive manner "I am guilty, and so is that man—he is as deep
in it as I am—if I am hung he ought to be hung, and if he is passed
over no man ought to be condemned by the Court—Lot was the
man who said to me on Gibbs' & Harper's Wharf, that nothing
could be done without fire, and that he had the combustibles for
it.[23]

A quantity of *slow match* which was found on Gibbs' & Harper's Wharf, and then in Court, was shewn to Captain C. L.
Black, Arsenal Keeper, who testified that the slow match produced to him resembled that in the Arsenal precisely, and he believed it to be a part of the same.

[*Note*. Lot was proved by the next witness to have been in
the employment of Mr. Peigne, who is often engaged in the Arsenal, and sometimes has servants with him there.]

NED, a Negro man belonging to Mr. Peigne, *a witness on behalf of the Prisoner,* testified as follows: I was at work with Lot on a house in my master's yard, when Vesey came there—Lot told him not to come in, that his master would not allow it—this was about the first of June.

THE COURT unanimously found Lot guilty, and passed upon him the sentence of death.

THE TRIAL OF ADAM, a Negro man, belonging to Mr. John Robertson—his owner attending.

Evidence

HARRY testified as follows: I met Adam at Bulkley's Farm, at a meeting there for rising against the whites. I know that he belongs to Gullah Jack's Company, and that he knew the meetings were for considering this subject—he did not tell me that he was one, but I heard him agree to be one in this purpose. I heard him acknowledge that he was in Gullah Jack's Company—he was one of the African Church.

BILLY gave the evidence which follows: Adam was twice at Bulkley's Farm, and once at Thayer's, to attend the meetings there —he belonged to the Gullah Company, to rise against the whites —he told me so—I heard him say so more than once.

THE COURT unanimously found Adam guilty, and passed upon him the sentence of death.

THE TRIAL OF JOHN, a Negro man, the property of Mr. John Robertson—his owner attending.

Evidence

HARRY testified as follows: John was engaged in this business —he belonged to Gullah Jack's Company, and was at the same meeting with Adam—he acknowledged that he belonged to the same company that I did—I met him but once at Bulkley's Farm— he belongs to the African Church.

BILLY gave the following evidence: John belongs to the Gullah Company—I heard him say so once—he was twice at the meetings at the farm.

THE COURT unanimously found John guilty, and passed upon him the sentence of death.

THE TRIAL OF BUTCHER, a Negro man, the slave of Mr. Gibbs.

Evidence

CHARLES testified as follows: Butcher belongs to the Company, and is engaged in this business—I met him at Bulkley's Farm—he is one who acknowledged in my presence that he was to rise against the whites. The object of the meeting at Bulkley's was to consider about this business. He belongs to the African Church.

BILLY's evidence was as follows: Butcher Gibbs belongs to Peter Ward's religious class.

Charles being the only witness against Butcher without any corroborating circumstances; the Court found him not guilty, but suggested to his owner the propriety of sending him away.

THE TRIAL OF SCIPIO, a Negro man, belonging to Mr. William Simms—his owner attending.

Evidence

PEIRAULT testified as follows: Scipio belongs to those who are to rise against the whites—he hired a horse from me on Saturday, the 8th of June, to go into the country, to get the Negroes to come down at the time the rising was to commence. I examined him myself, to see if he was one of my friends to fight against the whites. I met him at Mr. Aiken's lot, after the 8th, when we walked down together, as far as St. Philip and Wentworth Streets. We talked about this business. The third time I met him near Mr. Murphy's in King Street, on Sunday previous to the execution of Peter Poyas —I then said to Scipio, this thing was all up and now dead; Scipio replied, that all the people he had engaged were cowards and had drawn back, but that he was willing to go on as much as I myself could be.

Cross-examined by Mr. Simms—Scipio hired the horse, but aonther man took the horse who paid me $2 in part, and Adam a free man the remaining $1, the hire being $3—I don't know the man who took the horse, but I'd know him if I saw him again.

Re-examined—Scipio hired the horse and said he would send for it, and when the man came for the horse, he said Scipio had sent for the horse—when my horse was brought back the man was on my horse, and Scipio in company with him on another horse—my stable was near Flinn's Church, and they came from towards the lines, this was on Sunday Evening, 9th June. He belongs to the African Church.

MONDAY gave the evidence following: Jack Purcell told me that Scipio had gone into the country to collect people to come down.

CHARLES testified as follows: Monday told me pretty much what he has himself stated to the Court.

MR. WILLIAM SIMMS deposed as follows: Scipio is an orderly, sober, and industrious servant. I raised him, and we have worked together.

MRS. FICK, *a witness on behalf of the prisoner,* testified as follows: Scipio never gave to me any arms to keep for him or anything else—I have always thought him a steady, sober Negro, and never heard anything amiss of him.

Cross-examined by the Court—I never said that Scipio had left a sword or pistol with me.[24]

AGRIPPA, a Negro man belonging to Mrs. Perry, *a witness on behalf of the prisoner,* testified as follows: I requested Scipio to hire a horse for me to go into the country about the last day of the first week in June, mine being sick—Scipio carried me to the man from whom the horse was hired, I don't know the man. He and I went up on horseback to my mistress' plantation, on Horse-Savannah, where we went for my tools, and returned the next day, Sunday—this was all we went for.

Cross-examined by the Court: The man's name was Peirault, who lives on the green. I paid $2, and when I returned, paid him the $1—when I received the horse, Scipio was not with me. I had a pass, Scipio's name was not in my pass. I brought down my mallet, chisel, and axe. I left town on Saturday, about ten o'clock—about two weeks before this I was in the country.

As soon as Agrippa's examination ceased, Peirault was brought into Court, and immediately recognized him to be the man who had hired his horse, though he did not know his name. The Intendant then committed Agrippa for trial. In consequence of this charge against Agrippa, whose testimony was so important to Scipio, Mr. Simms requested the Court not to decide upon Scipio's case until Agrippa was tried, to which request the Court acceded. Agrippa was not tried until five days after, as his owner asked for time to send into the country and bring down some of the Negroes as witnesses who were on the plantation when Agrippa and Scipio arrived there. Agrippa's trial therefore was not the next after Scipio's; but as informing their decision on Scipio's case, the testimony given in Agrippa's was considered by the Court, it is thought advisable, that, in this publication, the report of the one trial should immediately succeed the other.

THE COURT unanimously found Scipio guilty, and passed upon him the following sentence: That he be imprisoned in the Work House of Charleston, until his master, under the direction of the City Council of Charleston, shall send him out of the limits of the United States, into which he is not to return under penalty of death.

THE TRIAL OF AGRIPPA, a Negro man belonging to Mrs. Perry, Mr. Edward Perry, the son of his owner—his counsel Benjamin F. Dunkin, Esq., Mr. Bartholomew Carrol, the friend of his owner, and Mr. William Simms attending.

Evidence

PEIRAULT testified as follows: On the 8th of June about ten o'clock, I met the prisoner, who said he was going into the country on some business, which would be good to me and good to him. On his return, I went to him, when after some conversation, he informed me that he had gone into the country to get men to join this insurrection, and that he had procured some men. He hired a horse from me, for which he paid me two dollars in my hand, and got security for the other dollar, which he afterwards paid through Adam Creighton—the price of the horse was three dollars.

Cross-examined by Mr. Dunkin—I never saw the prisoner before he came for the horse. I saw him the second time after he came from the country, when I examined him particularly, and he confessed that he had got some men to join in the insurrection.

Scipio Simms made the contract about the horse, and not the prisoner.

MR. EDWARD PERRY, *a witness on behalf of the prisoner,* deposed as follows: My mother allows the prisoner to keep a horse in the country where he usually resides—my mother informed me yesterday that his horse is lame, and has been so for some time. (The general ticket to work out in town or country from his mistress was produced in evidence.) The mother and father-in-law of the prisoner resides on my plantation, where the prisoner is in the habit of going about once a fortnight. There were not more than four or five able bodied Negroes on my plantation when the prisoner went for his tools.

Cross-examined by the Court—I have some near neighbors in the country at whose plantations there are many Negroes.

KITT, a Negro man, belonging to Mr. Perry, *a witness on behalf of the prisoner,* testified as follows: I was not present when Agrippa and Scipio arrived at the plantation—on my return home in the evening I met them. Agrippa's horse was so lame, that he once returned home on foot. He returned next day to town. I do not know Scipio. There were only four or five old persons on the plantation, the prime hands had come to town.

ROBIN, a Negro man, belonging to Mr. Perry, *a witness on behalf of the prisoner,* testified as follows: I went into the country with Scipio and Agrippa on Saturday morning. We arrived 'twixt three and four o'clock at Mr. Perry's plantation—we stopped on no plantation, nor to talk with any Negro on the way up. When on the plantation, Agrippa went to his house, and I to my mother's —about eight o'clock Agrippa and Scipio were in bed. Agrippa answered me when I came to the door, that he had gone to bed. I saw Agrippa about seven o'clock next day preparing to start—we started for town directly after breakfast, and did not stop on the way to speak to anyone, or at any plantation, and arrived in town about three o'clock. When we got down, I carried my horse where I got it—they went to carry theirs to the place they got them from. When on the plantation no strange Negroes were there, and I don't believe Agrippa or Scipio went off the plantation. They were working together in town, and as one could not go on without the other, as one had to go into the country for his tools, the other accompanied him. There were only about five men on the plantation. I was not with Agrippa and Scipio all the time that they were on the plantation.

Cross-examined by the Court—As soon as we arrived on the place, which was about three or four o'clock, we separated, and I did not see the others 'til about eight o'clock, when I called at their house, and found them in bed. From that time to 7 next morning, I did not see them.

Re-examined—I saw their horses frequently together with mine on the place before eight o'clock. I saw them together first about an hour after we arrived, and before eight o'clock they were put up. The nearest neighbor is about one mile and three quarters off.

DOLL, a Negro woman belonging to Mr. Perry, *a witness on behalf of the prisoner,* gave the following evidence: I was on the plantation when Scipio and Agrippa came up—they came up about an hour before sundown. I stayed at the big-house. Robin stopped at the big-house, and Agrippa and Scipio went on to Agrippa's mother's house. I did not see them again till next morning—about dusk they sent to me for some clauber. I saw them turn out their horses in the plantation directly after they arrived—and I saw their horses about sundown; they could not have gone out of the place without passing the big-house, unless they rode or walked through the field, and I did not see them pass. Mr. Singleton's is about a quarter of a mile distant (Mr. Carroll says about a mile and a half). The driver doesn't allow a horse to go through the field. I saw them next day after breakfast. There are no prime men on the plantation—all old or boys.

Cross-examined by the Court—There are about four taskable men on the plantation. Mr. Lee's plantation is not half as far as Singleton's.

LIDY, Agrippa's mother, testified as follows: I was at home when Agrippa and Scipio came to the plantation, not long before sundown—they turned their horses loose, then came in and sat down. They did not leave the house that night. Robin came there after they went to bed and called them, but no answer was given him. I got up before either of them next morning—and then I saw them laying as I left them at night—I don't think they could have gone out of the house and I not know it. They had no talk with the people on the plantation—they never left the house further than the door.

Cross-examined by the Court—I slept but little that night, my grandchild kept me awake. They carried away Agrippa's tools next day. Robin called three times, but no answer was given. They slept in the Hall and I in my room. The tools were some chisels and planes.

MR. EDWARD PERRY, again examined—The nearest plantation is about three quarters of a mile, but there is but one Negro man on it, the next nearest better than a mile.

JACK belonging to Mrs. Purcell testified that Scipio had spoken once to him about the insurrection.

THE COURT unanimously found Agrippa guilty, and passed upon him the following sentence: That he be imprisoned in the Work House of Charleston until his owner, under the direction of the City Council of Charleston shall send him out of the limits of the United States, into which he is not to return under penalty of death.

THE TRIAL OF DICK, a Negro man, the slave of Mr. William Simms—his owner attending.

Evidence

PEIRAULT testified as follows: Dick and I met on a Saturday evening in the cabinet maker's lot, next to Monday's, where we met on this business, Gullah Jack, George Vanderhorst, and Charles Drayton. Jack said he was going in his canoe into the country to get people—Dick said he belonged to Gullah Jack's Band, and said he was willing and ready like me. The second time we met at the corner of Market Street, we walked up King Street, and he told me he was ready at any time. The third time I met him between Crafts' and Smith's Wharf, and we sat down and conversed on this business. I again asked him, and he again said, he was ready at any time we were ready—I never met him anywhere else.

HARRY's evidence was as follows: Dick belonged to Gullah Jack's Company—I met him at Bulkley's Farm, and he confessed he was ready and willing to join—the meeting was about this business—he joined before I did.

Cross-examined by Mr. Simms—We all consulted together at the meeting, and all agreed—this was a little before this business broke out.

CHARLES testified as follows: I saw Dick in the lot of the mahogany shop near Monday's, attending one of the meetings—he was one of Jack's Company—this he said out of his own mouth, and that he was ready.

[*Note.* The prisoner confessed he was at this house, but said he went there to see someone.]

BILLY gave the following evidence: Dick was at three of the meetings on this business; once at Thayer's, and twice at Bulkley's Farm. He was there when they tried to fire off the pistol, and it went off in his hand.

[*Note.* The prisoner confessed he was sometimes at Bulkley's Farm, but said he went there to see Billy.]

Cross-examined by Mr. Simms—If I had not been there I would not have known of this business.

Re-examined by the Court—Whenever he came, he came in company with Gullah Jack, they met at the Farm to talk on this business.

THE COURT unanimously found Dick guilty, and passed upon him the sentence of death.

THE TRIAL OF BACCHUS, a Negro man, belonging to Mr. Benjamin Hammet—Francis S. Belzer, Esq., his owner's counsel, attending.

Evidence

PEIRAULT testified as follows: I engaged Bacchus myself to join in this business; he was one of my recruits. I carried him to Vesey's myself—he was willing to join. Bacchus took one keg of powder from his master and gave it to Vesey, who carried it to Monday's—he promised to give me a sword but did not do so.

Cross-examined by Mr. Belzer—Bacchus told me that he had carried the powder to Vesey.

MONDAY'S evidence was as follows: Bacchus told me he was

one in this business—he has often been at my shop and I had a keg of powder there he got. I saw him one night at Vesey's.

Cross-examined by Mr. Belzer—Bacchus and Peirault brought the powder to my shop.

CHARLES gave the following testimony: I met Bacchus at Monday's and at Vesey's. I was present when he brought the powder to Vesey's—he told me he had three swords, one for himself, one for Peirault, and one for Ned Bennett.

THE COURT unanimously found Bacchus guilty, and passed upon him the sentence of death.

Mr. Hammet, while he was not desirous that Bacchus should escape punishment, yet was anxious to save his life, and previous to his trial handed to the Court in writing a confession which Bacchus had made to him, and stated, that he came forward with this candid confession of Bacchus, in hopes of saving his life thereby; but that if the Court thought his case did not admit of a less punishment than death, he then requested that his confession should not be used against him. The Court after consultation determined to proceed to his trial. The following confession though not used against Bacchus is now given to the public:

Peirault, when hauling cotton from my master's store, told me in the yard, secretly, that he wanted me to go to Society with him. I asked what Society? He told me, never mind what Society, and said he would call for me that night—he did call and I went with him. Peirault carried me to Denmark Vesey's house, by Bennett's mill—there I met about twelve men, among whom was Monday Gell, and Smart Anderson. After I got in they fastened the gate—it was before nine o'clock. Denmark and Peirault took me to one side, Peirault told me they were going to tell me something; this was in another room, not before the gang. Denmark and Peirault said that they were going to turn to and fight the white people, and take the country, and that New Orleans was taken. I considered a long while, and they found me considering, and at last I said to Peirault I was very sorry he brought me there as I did not wish to belong to such a Society. Denmark Vesey said to me before Peirault, that the one who did not wish to join the Society must be put to death as an enemy—he told all the gang so after he went back with me into the room. Denmark told the gang, that they must meet at his house that night next week. Peirault told me to try and get powder, that the gang would throw in and make it up to me. They all threw in the night of meeting 12½ cents each, and I also. This money was thrown in to give a man to go into the country and bring down the country Negroes when they were all ready. When I asked about arms, and where they were, Denmark recommended to them to look through the town for the stores that had the most guns. Peirault then jumped up and said "Bacchus, don't you know where Captain Martindale's arms is?" I said, yes, my man, but you can't get them, and you had better drop this thing altogether. About two or three days after this last affair, Peirault came to me and told me that they had caught Denmark; he carried me down to Monday Gell. Monday and Peirault told me that Denmark said that if they caught him, he would tell nobody's name, and that I must not tell his, Peirault's name, nor Monday's, and they would not mention mine. I took the keg of powder out of the back store of my master, and carried it in a bag to Denmark, with a man belonging to Mr. Bennett who I believe is a blacksmith. Bennett's man met me at my master's gate. I suppose Pritchard's Gullah Jack and Peirault carried the powder to Monday from Denmark's house. In company with Denmark Vesey and Peirault, Denmark told me to get what arms I could. I said I could get one horseman's sword in a scabbard, which I took to Denmark's house. I also said I could get a pistol, but was afraid my master would miss it. Peirault told me never mind he could make me easy about it. I did take the pistol to Denmark's house with the sword, on Sunday night the 16th June. Denmark told me previously, I must not go home—this Denmark told at the meeting previous, and said they were to go up the road and meet the country Negroes. Last night, when I was put in the room in the Work House with Peirault, he told me Gullah Jack had buried the powder, and I think Peirault knows where it is. All the Negroes engaged in the plot were ordered by Denmark to leave their masters and go up the road. The night they carried me to Denmark, I was so frightened that I was obliged to say yes; for they threatened to kill everyone that did not wish to join. A large book like a Bible was open before them at Denmark's house; but I do not know whether it was to sign names in, or what purpose. At the first meeting at Denmark's, they asked me my name, and Peirault answered my name was Bacchus, belonging to Mr. Hammet—Denmark asked me which Hammet? I said Benjamin Hammet, the gentleman who sued Lorenzo Dow.

The week after Denmark was dead, Peirault told me to mind and keep myself ready, that they intended to come up at the corner where the arms of the Neck Company is kept, and I said very well; they were to take the arms, and I was to assist them, they were to break open the door. Monday Gell can tell who is at the head of this last arrangement—I believe Peirault knows all about it. Gullah Jack was to distribute the powder among us. Peirault told me that they had a blacksmith to make daggers for this party, and that they had made some. On Sunday, 16th June, he told me, *they had three or four hundred daggers*—he told me on the 11th July, the night I was committed, that I must not tell his name or anything about it. This was the reason I was afraid to tell or make a confession to my master, Mr. Hammet, on this morning, the 12th July. Peirault is the fellow that has brought me into this scrape. A fellow about my size, a dark black skin Negro, who I believe is called Charles, took me up the road just before you come to the forks of the road, on Meeting Street, to a farm. The house on the farm has a piazza on the top; Charles told the Negro man on the farm, "mind next Sunday the business is to be done," (meaning to kill the white people); and that the Negroes from the country were to stop at this farm. Denmark Vesey and his party from town was to go there to the farm to meet the Negroes from the country. I solemnly declare as to being brought into this scrape; and that Peirault is the one who enticed me into it. At the first meeting at Denmark Vesey's house, on the breaking up of the meeting Denmark said—"Friends, you all throw in seven pence apiece, those who have got it, it is to make up for a friend to pay his wages to his master, before he went into the country to bring the people down."

At the meeting at Denmark Vesey's the first time I was there, I saw a fat black fellow whom I think was Denmark's son. He looked very much like Denmark, had a full face, and he could read, as he showed Monday Gell the large book on the table, and said to him, showing him the leaf of the book, "see here, they are making real game at we." Monday looked at the book and said nothing.

Denmark took me to one side and said, "we shan't be slaves to these damn rascals any longer. We must kill everyone that we can get hold of, and drive the rest out of the city." No one was with me when I was requested by Charles (whom he calls Charles Drayton now) to go to the farm at the forks of the roads; when Charles set out to go there, he came from Monday Gell's house, met me, and carried me to Monday's. Monday was to go with Charles to the farm, but put it off on account of having a hog to kill, and said to Charles, let this friend go with you; and Charles and I went to the farm. When we went to the farm, Charles asked a Negro woman on the farm, if the old daddy was home, and she called him. This old daddy is an African, marked on both sides of his face. Charles took him in the stable, and also myself, and told him about the country Negroes coming there. The fellow who helped me to carry the powder belonged to Bennett I think, because I have seen this man in Bennett's blacksmith shop at the mill, years before this. Peirault told me that they had *two or three hundred bayonets made already*—Peirault is a blacksmith. I believe Monday knows as well as Peirault where the arms and bayonets are. Monday said they were to have mounted horsemen—that many draymen belonged to it who had horses. At Denmark's house they all rose up and swore, lifting up the right hand, saying, "we will not tell if we are found out, and if they kill us we will not tell on anyone." Denmark said they must all say so, and that they did say so. Denmark told me that he gave the sword to Peirault, and Peirault gave it to a man named Caesar. I know no other Caesar but a drayman named Caesar Smith—a tall Negro, an African, who is an intimate acquaintance of Peirault's, and who is often at the stable where Peirault keeps his horses. Peirault told me that French Negroes were among them—Denmark said country born, Africans and all kinds joined. Monday and Peirault appeared to be the intimate friends of Denmark, he thought a heap of them. Denmark took the pistol for himself, it was given to him in his own hand. Those meetings were held at Denmark's house, where he had a black wife—two or three women were at the house ironing.

JOHN, a Negro man, the slave of Mr. J. L. Enslow, pleaded guilty. His owner, who was present, stated to the Court, that

John was willing to make the only reparation in his power for his conduct, and would reveal all the information he was in possession of relative to the insurrection. The Court informed John that he might state whatever he had to say, but as they would not make him any promise, he must not make confessions in hopes of pardon. John said he would state all he knew of the intended insurrection, and proceeded to make the following confession:

Monday Gell led me into it, and took me to Vesey's; there was a large meeting. Vesey told the people, the meeting was to rise up and fight the white people for their liberty. We always went to Monday's house afterwards—Monday did all the writing. I heard that they were trying all round the country *from Georgetown and Santee, round about to Combahee,* to get people. Peter Poyas was also there, he was one. Peter named Poyas' plantation where he went to meet. Bellisle Yates I have seen at the meetings, and Adam Yates, and Naphur Yates, and Dean Mitchell, and Caesar Smith, and George a Stevedore. At Vesey's they wanted to make a collection to make pikes for the country people, but the men had then no money. Monday Gell said Peirault was one to get horses to send men into the country. I heard that a blacksmith was to make pikes. Jack McNeil is engaged. I have seen them all at Monday's. Jack said he was one and would try to get men. The plan was to take the Arsenal and Guard Houses for arms, and not to fire the town unless they failed. Monday was writing a letter to Santo Domingo to go by a vessel lying at Gibb's and Harper's Wharf—the letter was about the sufferings of the blacks, and to know if the people of Santo Domingo would help them if they made an effort to free themselves. He was writing this letter in March, I am not certain of the time. Peirault was present when Monday wrote the letter, and also a Painter named Prince Righton. I have seen Pompey Haig at Monday's, but he neither assented nor dissented. Jerry Cohen was at Vesey's, and said to me he was one. I heard from Vesey and Monday that they had engaged men from the country— Peter Poyas said he had sent into the country to his brother to engage men who would send him an answer. A party was to attack the Guard House and Arsenal—another the Arsenal on the Neck —another to attack the Naval Store on Mey's Wharf—another to attack the Magazine—another to meet at Lightwood's Alley, and then try to cut off the Companies from meeting at their places of rendezvous. I belong to the African Congregation. On Saturday, the 15th June, a man was to be sent into the country to bring down the people, and Rolla was to command (the country people from Ashley River) at the Bridge, Ned Bennett and John Horry to meet at Mr. Horry's corner, and Batteau to come down with Vesey's party.

THE COURT having used John as a witness in the subsequent trials, passed upon him the following sentence—"That he be imprisoned in the Work House of Charleston, until his master, under the direction of the City Council of Charleston shall send him out of the limits of the United States, into which he is not to return under penalty of death."

THE TRIAL OF WILLIAM, a Negro man, the property of Mr. Job Palmer—his owner attending.

Evidence

MONDAY testified as follows: William belongs to the association to rise against the whites. He and Vesey, and Jack Glenn have been at my shop together—they were talking on this business, and he said he would do as much as any other man, and confessed he had joined. Vesey seemed to regard him as one of his men, and to feel confidence in him. He and I were to be in the same band under Vesey—he was often in my shop talking on this business, and never showed any disposition to be off—this was before the first execution.

Cross-examined by Mr. Palmer—The time that Vesey, Glenn, and William were at my shop, was when Vesey said there was but one Minister who preached the gospel. Sometimes he came to my shop alone—the first time he came in he asked for the newspaper—the first conversation he had was about the rising.

CHARLES gave the following evidence: William is engaged in the insurrection—he said to Vesey in Monday's shop that Vesey must not think that he would not fight; that he would fight as well as another. I met him opposite to the Circular Church, on Dr. Simons' step, and he then said it was a shame they should allow the men to be hanged; *that he was ready to join in rescuing them from the gallows*—this was the Sunday previous to Vesey's being hanged, about 2 P.M.

Cross-examined by Mr. Palmer—I knew him long before; I met him just after William Paul was taken up at Vesey's. (See Monday Gell's confession, in which he says, that William promised Vesey to enlist as many men as he could, on page 68.)

THE COURT unanimously found William guilty, and passed upon him the sentence of death.

[*Note.* His Excellency the Governor has pardoned William, upon condition that his Master transports him beyond the limits of the United States.]

THE TRIAL OF SEYMOUR, a Negro man, belonging to Mr. William F. Kunhardt—his owner attending.

Evidence

PEIRAULT testified as follows: I met Seymour once at Monday's with Smart Anderson, where he acknowledged he was one to rise, and that he belonged to Monday's Company. I met him afterwards at the exchange, where we talked of this business, and he was as much one as myself.

MONDAY gave the following evidence: Seymour is one in this business—he brought to my shop about two months ago a raccoon skin to make a cap of, and he then agreed to join us; he and Joe Jore are particular friends. I met him afterwards in Meeting Street, where he again said he was willing.

THE COURT unanimously found Seymour guilty, and passed upon him the sentence of death; but recommended to the Governor that he should be pardoned upon condition that he be transported out of the limits of the United States.

THE TRIAL OF NAPHUR, ADAM, AND BELLISLE, three Negro men, belonging to the Estate of Joseph Yates deceased—Jacob Axson, Esq., attending as their counsel.

Evidence

PEIRAULT testified as follows: Bellisle or Blarney was engaged in this business. I met him at Crafts' North Wharf—this was the first meeting. The second meeting was at the corner of the scale house, on Smith's Wharf. He told me that the night the blacks were to rise, he would engage the people of Mr. Yates to sleep with himself at Mr. Mitchell's, while his people slept on Smith's Wharf, where they would commence the fight. Adam and Naphur met at Bulkley's Farm where we met on this business; there were Vesey, Monday, Charles, and Smart. There I told them they had done the worst thing they could do to engage these people, for that all Charleston would know it the next day (the rope-walk people got them to join). Adam and Naphur there acknowledged they had joined. On the 16th I saw Adam in the street, when he said he was going up the road to meet the country and Neck people, where he intended to remain that night, and come down with those people.

Bellisle belongs to the African Church; they are all Africans.

Cross-examined by Mr. Axson—Naphur and Adam came up to the farm about twelve o'clock in the day on Sunday, and stayed there 'til four o'clock—this was a Sunday in May. Every man in the house agreed to join to rise against the whites—the meeting was for this express purpose. After Peter Poyas and the others were convicted, Bellisle and I came out of the shop together to talk on this business, and I said we must rise and not let these people be hanged, and he said yes, we must do so; this was after he said to me he would get the people to sleep at Mr. Mitchell's shop on 16th June, when they were to rise. Adam told me that Charles Drayton had told him to go up the road on the 16th June, and stay there until the alarm was given, then come down with the Neck and country people. Adam and Naphur came up to the farm together—the Sunday was about the middle of May.

CHARLES gave the following evidence: Naphur, Adam, and Bellisle are all in this business. I met Adam and Naphur at Bulkley's Farm, where we met on this business, and where they acknowledged that their hearts were in this business. I met Bellisle in the streets, where he told me he belonged to it. I have also met him often at Monday's, where he talked of it, he said he was one of the army, and ready and willing to go out.

Cross-examined by Mr. Axson—Naphur and Adam at the farm, said when the rising commenced they were ready. Vesey was there and spoke to the whole, and all who agreed to rise against the whites were to hold up their hands, and Naphur and Adam held up theirs with the others.

JOHN, Mr. Enslow's slave, testified as follows: I know the prisoners; they are as much in the plot as I am, and I am in the plot. I have met them all at Monday's. Adam gave a knife to Monday to make a scabbard which he intended to use as a dagger; the knife was such a one as the riflemen wear. I have heard Naphur at Monday's agree to join. I belong to Monday's company. Bellisle said he was in it. Adam and I have often spoken on the same subject—we all agreed to rise against the whites and fight for our freedom.

Cross-examined—I saw Adam deliver the knife to Monday, and say make a scabbard if this will do—we all agreed at Monday's to join.

MONDAY gave the testimony following: The prisoners were in the habit of coming into my shop to talk on this business. I first met Naphur and Adam at Bulkley's Farm. Adam brought to me a long knife to make a scabbard which he intended to use in the business. They belonged to my side which was Vesey's division—I delivered to him afterwards the knife.

Cross-examined by Mr. Axson—Naphur was but once in my shop—Bellisle and Adam often at the farm. Denmark Vesey explained his plan to all present, and on the proposition to agree, all assented. I met Naphur once at Bulkley's Farm, where as well as at my shop he expressly agreed to join.

[*Note.* Two other witnesses were ready to be produced against the prisoners, but the Court thought it unnecessary to examine them, as they could not testify to any new facts.]

THE COURT unanimously found Naphur, Adam, and Bellisle guilty, and passed upon them the sentence of death.

THE TRIAL OF DUBLIN, a Negro man, the property of Mr. Thomas Morris—Mr. C. G. Morris attending.

Evidence

PEIRAULT testified as follows: Dublin said to me that William Garner had engaged him to join against the whites—he belongs to the African Church.

CHARLES testified as follows: Dublin told me one day he heard of it but that was all.

THE COURT unanimously found Dublin guilty, and passed upon him the sentence of death, but recommended to the Governor to pardon him upon condition that he be transported out of the limits of the United States.

THE TRIAL OF CHARLES, a Negro man, belonging to Mr. Samuel Billings—his owner attending.

Evidence

JOHN testified as follows: Charles belongs to this business. We spoke on it at Monday's—he said that when we were ready he would come out and join us. I met him twice at Monday's, and both times he said so. After Peter was taken up, I met him on Edmonston's Wharf, and he said the people were beginning to be frightened, and we had better say as little as possible about it.

PEIRAULT's evidence was as follows: I met him at Monday's where I heard him say he was a horseman—I heard him say he was ready and willing.

MONDAY gave the following evidence: He told me once that William Garner had spoke to him about a horse, but I don't know that he was one of us—he was frequently at my shop to get harnesses mended, and he there conversed on this subject, and he appeared willing to join, and said he had joined.

CHARLES testified as follows: I have met him often, and he acknowledged he was one. Jack Glenn he said was to have slept at his master's livery stables the night of the rising, to assist in saddling the horses for the company.

[*Note.* Other witnesses were ready to testify to the same effect, but it was thought unnecessary to examine them as they would testify to no new fact.]

MR. BILLINGS testified to Charles' general good character.

THE COURT unanimously found Charles guilty, and passed upon him the sentence of death.

THE TRIAL OF PRINCE, a Negro man, the property of Miss Righton—Mr. Joseph Righton, attending.

Evidence

JOHN testified as follows: I have seen Prince in Monday's shop when Monday was reading the letter to Santo Domingo—he must have heard Monday. The brother of the steward of the vessel who was to carry the letter to Santo Domingo was a General, as I understand, in Santo Domingo.

MONDAY gave the evidence following: I can't say that Prince was engaged—he came once to my shop and then agreed to join, but I have not seen him since, and as he did not come back to say whether he would continue so or not, I therefore did not put his name down to the list. This was long before the 16th June—I then read the list of names to him, but not the letter to Santo Domingo—there were three other persons there.

Cross-examined by Mr. Righton—he came there without any appointment.

CHARLES testified as follows: I saw him once in Monday's shop, but don't know anything against him.

HARRY stated that he knew nothing against Prince.

THE COURT unanimously found Prince not guilty—but suggested to his owner to send him away.

THE TRIAL OF PETER, an elderly Negro man, belonging to Mrs. Cooper—Captain Sears Hubbell, attending.

Evidence

JOHN testified as follows: I have met Peter at Monday's, where he signified his consent, and said he was willing to join; this was about two months ago.

MONDAY gave the following evidence: Peter said he would join. I met him once at Vesey's, and he there said by word of mouth that he was willing to join; this was previous to the 16th June (the prisoner is a Guinea Negro). He has passed my shop driving his cart, but did not come in.

PEIRAULT testified as follows: Vesey told me to tell Peter he wanted to see him; I told him and he said he would go, and did go; but I did not know what passed there; I don't know that he agreed; I came out of Vesey's and left him there; Vesey sent me to him on this business; I only delivered my message.

Cross-examined by Captain Hubbell—At Vesey's I met Monday there too.

MR. HUBBELL deposed that Peter has borne a good character, and is an inoffensive man.

THE COURT unanimously found Peter guilty, and passed upon him the sentence of death; but in consideration of his age, recommended to the Governor to pardon him upon condition that he be transported out of the limits of the United States.

[*Note.* His Excellency the Governor has pardoned Peter on condition of his receiving twenty lashes.]

THE TRIAL OF GEORGE, a Negro man, the property of Mr. Bampfield—his owner attending.

Evidence

JOHN testified as follows: I met George at Monday's, where he said, that if all the men in the room were of one mind, he would make a remark—they said we are; he then said, I have spoken to two men who agreed, and mentioned their names; when Monday said for God sake let them alone or they will betray us; (the prisoner on being asked if he belonged to the African Church said, he did belong to the African Church, but they turned him out for keeping a girl).

MONDAY's evidence was as follows: George was once in my shop; the conversation related by John Enslow did not take place; every day there were numbers in my shop on this business; he was often in my shop.

PEIRAULT testified as follows: I met George once at Monday's; George did agree to join as much as I did; I did not hear him say anything about engaging two men to join—this meeting was expressly on this business. I met him afterwards in the market, when he said the guards were too strong, let the business lay still; I have not talked to him since anyone was taken up on this business.

CHARLES testified as follows: Monday told me that George was one.

THE COURT unanimously found George guilty, and passed

upon him the sentence of death; but recommended to the Governor to pardon him upon condition that he be sent out of the limits of the United States.

THE TRIAL OF JEMMY, a Negro man, belonging to Mrs. Clement—his two young masters present.

Evidence

MONDAY testified as follows: Jemmy is engaged in this business; he belongs to my company, and he agreed in my shop. He said he would like to know when this business would begin, as he had engaged some people in the country where his wife lived, and he would have to bring them down. He has often come to my shop and held conversations on this subject, and confessed he was willing and had joined.

PEIRAULT gave the following evidence: I saw Jemmy at Monday's—he knew of it before me, for at that time he was talking on this business, and it was the first time I had heard of it. He was one—he was willing—he belongs to the African Church.

CHARLES testified as follows: Jemmy told me himself in Monday's shop, that he was one. He one day brought to me on the market wharf two or three men, who he said had agreed to join, and belonged to the country. These men said they had joined, and were to carry the news into the country (Jemmy has a wife at Mrs. Moore's, in St. Thomas' Parish)—this was after Peter was taken up, but before his execution.

THE COURT unanimously found Jemmy guilty, and passed upon him the sentence of death.

THE TRIAL OF JERRY, a Negro man, the slave of Mr. M. Cohen.

Evidence

JOHN testified as follows: I met Jerry at Vesey's, and at Monday's. He agreed and said he was one, and joined in the object of the meeting, which was to plan measures against the whites— we have often spoken on this business. At Vesey's where we met were present, Monday, Charles, Rolla, Ned, Peirault, Batteau,

Smart, and Jack Glenn, and near 30 men in all. They then handed round the hat to make collections to purchase pikes; they were to be provided with dark lanterns to enter stores for arms. *Vesey said one hundred pikes were made by a black man who worked by himself;* they also wanted money to pay that black man's wages to his mistress. After Vesey was taken I was afraid to speak on the subject.

MONDAY gave the evidence following: Jerry was often in my shop, and confessed he was one; his name was on my list with his consent. I did not meet him at Vesey's; he said when we were consulting who should take a lead, said he would be a leader. He was not there when money was collected to procure lanterns. I did not go to the meeting that night 'til eight o'clock.

PEIRAULT testified as follows: Jerry was at Vesey's when they made a collection; I am not certain, but think that Monday was present—Monday *was* there. John Enslow was also there; the collection was for purchasing spears. Jerry did say we had better stop this business, but still he was willing to go on if we went on.

THE COURT unanimously found Jerry guilty, and passed upon him the sentence of death.

THE TRIAL OF DEAN, a Negro man belonging to Mr. Jas. Mitchell—his owner attending.

Evidence

PEIRAULT testified as follows: I have seen Dean at Vesey's, where he agreed as much as myself—we met purposely to make *a collection for spears.* I heard him say he had joined, and no one would be allowed to enter that house if he was not one. He belongs to the African Church.

Cross-examined by Mr. Mitchell—John Enslow summoned him to attend the meeting.

JOHN testified as follows: I first told Dean about it—he told me afterwards he saw the thing was going on well, and he was glad of it. I asked him if he would like to go to Vesey's meetings, and he said yes, and went with me. He put in money at Vesey's, I saw him do it; Jack Glenn handed the hat round. We afterwards conversed, and he was always of the same mind. He was on the night of the rising to meet at Vesey's, and march down with his party.

MONDAY confirmed John's testimony as far as it relates to Dean's meeting at Vesey's and as to what passed there.

THE COURT unanimously found Dean guilty, and passed upon him the sentence of death.

THE TRIAL OF ISAAC, a Negro man, the property of Mr. Wm. Harth—his owner attending.

Evidence

MONDAY testified as follows: Isaac was engaged in this business; he told me so himself. After Mingo was taken up, he told me that Mingo would get clear if Edwin Paul did not testify against him. He said also, that he belonged to the horse company. Mingo told me that his brother was one too.

Cross-examined by Mr. Harth—I conversed with him directly after Mingo was taken up.

WILLIAM testified that Edwin did positively say, all Mr. Harth's people were engaged in it.

CHARLES testified that Monday told him Isaac was engaged.

THE COURT unanimously found Isaac guilty, and passed upon him the sentence of death; but recommended to the Governor to pardon him upon condition that he be sent out of the limits of the United States.

THE TRIAL OF JOHN, a Negro man belonging to Mrs. Taylor —Mr. James Drummond attending.

Evidence

CHARLES testified as follows: John told me one Monday morning, previous to the 16th of June, that all the horses were ready, but the Patrol was so vigilant, they could not come out.

Cross-examined by Mr. Drummond—I understood the horses to be intended for the insurrection. This conversation took place at my master's gate—he was as willing as myself and he did not refuse. I only conversed with him but once, and then he told me the horses were ready for the insurrection. William Garner told me that John was engaged in this affair.

THE COURT unanimously found John not guilty, but suggested to his owner to send him away. Mr. Drummond gave John an excellent character.

THE TRIAL OF PIERRE LEWIS, a Negro man, the slave of Mr. Chappeau—his owner attending.

Evidence

CHARLES testified as follows: On Sunday, when the Guards were out, Pierre Lewis told me that something serious would happen, but that I was a countryborn, and he was afraid to trust me. This was on the 16th June.

THE COURT unanimously found Pierre Lewis not guilty, and discharged him.

THE TRIAL OF JACK, a Negro man, belonging to Mr. Neil McNeil—Mr. McKenzie, his owner's co-partner, attending.

Evidence

MONDAY testified as follows: Jack belongs to this conspiracy, and with his consent I placed him on my list. He has been frequently at my shop, where Denmark Vesey has often seen him; but he was never at my shop at any appointed meeting. He came here about 7 years of age from Africa, and belongs to the African Church. He is one of my company.

CHARLES testified as follows: I have met Jack at Monday's several times, and heard him in his presence acknowledge that he belonged to this conspiracy. After the execution of the first six, Jack appeared to be alarmed, and to regret that he had joined. We had several conversations and he always appeared to exhibit the same feelings.

PEIRAULT said: I know the prisoner, but not that he is engaged.

JOHN testified as follows: I have seen Jack often in Monday's shop and he has acknowledged in his presence and mine, that he had joined; he has spoken to me often on the subject in the streets, and was always willing.

THE COURT unanimously found Jack guilty, and passed upon him the sentence of death.

THE TRIAL OF CAESAR, a Negro man belonging to Mrs. Smith
—Mr. McDow attending for his owner.

Evidence

JOHN testified as follows: Caesar is engaged and confessed it
to me; I have often seen him at Monday's. He is a native of
Africa and belongs to the African Church. He told me sometimes
in the street he was engaged. After the execution of Vesey he
appeared fearful of the consequences.

Cross-examined by Mr. McDow—I saw him twice at Monday's before the 16th of June and once after.

MONDAY's evidence was as follows: Caesar was one of the
party, and I placed his name on my list. He was always willing
to join, there was no man more so.

Cross-examined by Mr. McDow—He engaged sometime before the affair was discovered. He was as zealous as myself—he
was at my shop often.

CHARLES testified as follows: Caesar acknowledged to me at
Monday's, that he was engaged, and also several times in the
street.

Cross-examined by Mr. McDow—I saw him after the execution of Vesey, and he appeared of the same mind.

THE PRISONER admitted in his defence, that he had frequent
conversations on this subject with the witness, but denied that he
had joined.

THE COURT unanimously found Caesar guilty, and passed upon
him the sentence of death.

THE TRIAL OF PRINCE GRAHAM, a free black man—Mr.
Jones attending as his friend.

Evidence

MONDAY testified as follows: Prince Graham is engaged in
this conspiracy and belongs to William Garner's Company—he
acknowledged he belonged to it, but did not wish to have his name
down, as he was a free man. He confessed he belonged to William
Garner's Company—he was not at my shop.

Cross-examined by Mr. Jones—he said he had a long one, a

horseman's sword provided for this purpose. He belonged to the cavalry and was one of the African Church. He never was with Denmark Vesey or attended any of the meetings. He told me he was to be an officer, William Garner had made him one.

CHARLES gave the following evidence: Monday and myself met Prince Graham one night coming out of Dr. Ramsay's yard with Quash Harleston—he said that he was as willing as anybody. After Morris Brown had returned from the North, he said he did not wish much to do with it as he was a free man, and had denied it to Morris Brown, who inquired if he was one—this was after Peter was taken up. Morris Brown returned before the 16th of June.

FRANK testified as follows: Vesey called at the house of Prince Graham one day in my company, and was informed by his wife that he was not at home. I afterwards met him and he asked why Vesey had called on him—I said to go into the country—he replied I cannot go, as I have nothing to do with this conspiracy. This was I think before the 16th of June.

PEIRAULT's evidence was as follows: I only conversed with Prince Graham once in company with Quash Harleston, when he said, if Monday had told him of it a little sooner he would have joined; but now he had not time to prepare himself for it— this was at Prioleau's Wharf.

PRINCE GRAHAM's statement and defence was as follows: I met William Garner who told me he held a commission in the horse, and if I would join, he would resign in my favor; which I refused to do. When in New York, I first learned that Denmark Vesey and others were to be hung for an attempt to raise an insurrection. As I had been spoken to and asked to join in this before I left Charleston, I considered well whether I had ever said or done anything which could bring me into trouble if I returned; but as I could not reproach myself with having done so, I thought I need not fear to come on. As I was a free man, and could have stayed in New York if I pleased, I certainly would not have been such a fool as to run myself into such danger if I was in any way engaged in the plot.

THE COURT found Prince Graham guilty, and passed upon him the following sentence: That he be imprisoned in the Work

House of Charleston for one month, and then be transported by sea out of the State of South Carolina, by the first opportunity, into which he is not to return under penalty of death.

The prisoner at his own request, was transported to Africa on board of a vessel which sailed from Charleston.

THE TRIAL OF BILLY, a Negro man, the property of Mr. Robinson—William Crafts, Esq., attending as his counsel.

Evidence

PEIRAULT testified as follows: Billy was engaged in this business. On the 16th of June he and I went to Vesey's in the afternoon. This day he said we must raise today, nothing must put it back. We there met Gullah Jack and Tom Russel—Smart Anderson got him to join. I met him afterwards, on Sunday at his own house. Billy agreed as much as myself. At his house, after Vesey and the others were taken, he said Jack would get more men, and then we would rise. We there spoke of rescuing Vesey and the others, and Billy agreed—he is an African.

Cross-examined by Mr. Crafts—We stopped first at Monday's and then went to Vesey's. On the day of the execution, on the Bay, Billy asked me what I was doing there—why I was not on the green to get men to rescue those to be hung.

The Prisoner's Defence: Mr. Davenport, Mr. Crafts, Mr. Tyler, and Mr. Davis testified to Billy's good character.

MR. TYLER deposed as follows: I believe that Peirault was one of those who were speaking with Billy before my door. At another time, within a few days Peirault took away in his dray from before my store some damaged corn sold him by Billy. I have powder in cannisters in my store, which Billy might have stolen if he chose to do so, but I have not missed any.

MRS. MILLER deposed as follows: I live in a house in Elliott Street, there are two rooms on a floor—the first occupied by Mr. Howe, the back by me. Billy occupies a room above my kitchen, and no one can go into his room without passing through my kitchen; I never saw Peirault go into Billy's room, or in my yard. Billy has lived in that room for three years.

Mr. Miller, Mr. J. W. Howe, T. Dexter, and Mrs. Mitchell, say they never saw Peirault in Billy's house.

PEIRAULT was called back by Mr. Crafts and examined as to Billy's residence, which he described exactly as Mrs. Miller had done.

SMART, belonging to Mr. Anderson, was examined on behalf of the State and testified as follows: Billy was engaged in this business—Caesar Smith said to me in Billy's presence, that Billy had joined. Billy told me that he was willing to take a part three or four days after this—he told me after that, that he was one.

Cross-examined by Mr. Crafts—I did not tell Peirault I had got Billy to join, but that Caesar had.

Re-examined—I have never been at Billy's house.

THE COURT unanimously found Billy guilty, and passed upon him the sentence of death.

[*Note.* His Excellency the Governor has pardoned Billy, upon condition, that his master transport him beyond the limits of the United States.]

THE TRIAL OF JOHN VINCENT, a Negro man belonging to Mr. Cruckshanks—Mr. Cornhill, one of the firm of D. Parish & Co. which had for some time hired him, attending.

Evidence

MONDAY testified as follows: John told me himself he had joined in this business—this was in my shop. I frequently conversed with him on this subject. He once belonged to the African Church. Before the 16th June he told me he had a mold, and that he was making balls—this was about three weeks before the 16th. After the 16th he said he was ready still.

Cross-examined by Mr. Cornhill—He said he would give me some bullets; he said his master, that he was staying with, was going to the North on Monday, the 18th, and if he would go on Saturday before, 'twould be better.

CHARLES gave the following evidence: I have often talked with John in Monday's shop on this subject, where he said he was willing; he was one, and belonged to the horse company. I have seen him at Monday's three or four times; he said the gentleman he was staying with wanted him to go to the North, but he said he wanted to stay and see the frolic over first.

Cross-examined by Mr. Cornhill—I think it was in his own room in an Alley from Church Street, viz. Elliott Street, that he told me about his master; this was the Sunday afternoon before Vesey was executed (30th June). Mr. Cornhill states that the prisoner did live in Elliott Street.

MR. CORNHILL gave to the prisoner the very best character.

MR. KER BOYCE deposed as follows: I went to D. Parish on Saturday, 15th June, who was going to the North on Monday. Mr. Parish asked John what was the matter, that he looked as if he had lost his mother. John's looks then were such, that after I heard of this affair next day, I could not but think that John was concerned, I advised Mr. Parish to question him about it.

THE COURT unanimously found John Vincent guilty, and passed upon him the sentence of death.

[*Note.* His Excellency the Governor has pardoned John Vincent, upon condition that his master transport him beyond the limits of the United States.]

THE TRIAL OF JACOB STAGG, a mulatto man, the slave of Mr. J. Lancaster—his owner and Joseph Clark, Esq., his counsel, attending.

Evidence

PEIRAULT testified as follows: Jacob and I talked together about April last in Monday's shop on this business, and I found that he knew of it before me; Smart Anderson and George Walker were there. On 15th June, we talked together near Flinn's Church, where I told him that Vesey said, tomorrow the people would come from the country, and we must rise; and he agreed to do so. I have met him frequently at Monday's.

Cross-examined by Mr. Clark—At Monday's shop on a rainy day he said he was engaged in the business, and belonged to the foot company; near Flinn's Church he said he was ready. *It was agreed to rise in July at first, as at that time the white people go to the North and to Sullivan's Island, and the City would then be thin of men;* but in consequence of the first arrest of Peter Poyas, it was altered and fixed for the 16th June. Monday told me in his shop in Jacob's presence, that he Jacob had joined.

MONDAY gave the following evidence: Jacob agreed to join with my company in my shop; he asked me for a sword, and when I said I had none to give him, he said, that he would get a scythe and make a sword out of it. Vesey had met him at my shop and talked with him on this business; he sometimes came to my shop and always said he was ready and willing. He first came to my shop about four months ago when it was cold weather. One rainy day he was a long time in my shop talking on this business, when he said he was engaged in painting the house; there were there several persons present. He said he would be ready when they rose.

Cross-examined by Mr. Clark—I don't remember that I told anyone that he had joined. Vesey mentioned his plans and arrangements, and what he was going to do in Jacob's presence; Jacob frequented my shop, and I have known him for four or five years.

CHARLES testified as follows: I have seen Jacob at Monday's when Vesey was there, but don't know that he had joined; I went out of the shop and left them talking; he said he was tired of paying wages.

Cross-examined by Mr. Clark—I have known of this about two months.

MR. LANCASTER AND MR. WHITNEY gave Jacob a good character, and so did Mr. Stagg.

Jacob had a wife at Dr. Ramsay's, and was always at home at night.

THE PRISONER stated that Monday read daily the newspapers, and told him that Congress was going to set them free (alluding to the Missouri question); he said, to hear about that carried him to Monday's.

THE COURT unanimously found Jacob Stagg guilty, and passed upon him the sentence of death.

THE TRIAL OF SAM, a Negro man, belonging to Mr. Henry Barnstile—his owner's friend, Mr. Wadsworth, attending.

Evidence

PEIRAULT testified that Sam agreed to join, and we have often talked together about it; he often said he was one and was ready.

THE COURT, as they placed great reliance on Peirault's veracity, unanimously found Sam guilty, and passed upon him the following sentence, That he be imprisoned in the Work House of Charleston, until his master, under the direction of the City Council of Charleston, shall send him out of the limits of the United States, into which he is not to return under the penalty of death.

THE TRIAL OF TOM, a Negro man, the property of Mr. William M. Scott—his owner attending.

Evidence

MONDAY testified as follows: I told Tom of the business, and he joined; he was often at my shop talking on this business; he was willing, had joined, and said he was making ready. He was of the same mind after the 16th June; he belongs to the African Church.

Cross-examined by Mr. Scott—It is about three months since I spoke to him about it; the first time it was fixed to commence on the second Sunday in July, and Vesey afterwards altered it to the 16th June.

PEIRAULT gave the following evidence: Tom told me he was engaged in this business with his own mouth, and was willing; he told me the day that Monday was taken of the circumstance and said, *the more we stand still, the more of us will be taken;* he belonged to Monday's company.

CHARLES testified as follows: I have heard Tom and Monday often in Monday's shop talking on this business, and heard him assent to the business; he spoke boldly.

MR. HARTH stated that the prisoner had a wife in his yard, and bore a good character; I have examined his trunk but found no arms.

THE COURT unanimously found Tom guilty, and passed upon him the sentence of death.

THE TRIAL OF DENBOW, a Negro man, the slave of Mr. J. N. Martin—his owner and William Crafts, Esq., as his counsel attending.

Evidence

MONDAY testified as follows: Denbow's name was on my list; he agreed to join about three months ago. Vesey has met him and spoke to him in my shop as one of his men; he was often at my shop. After Peter was taken up he said he was just as much for it as ever; he told me that Stephen Smith told him he belonged to one of the party. None ever told me to put their names down on my list, but those who positively agreed, I put their names down myself. Prisoner *did* belong to the African Church, but now to the Lutheran.

PEIRAULT testified as follows: I met Denbow at Monday's, speaking about this business, about two or three months ago, where he said, that so many persons were knowing of this business, we had better let it alone.

CHARLES DRAYTON testified that he had met Denbow at Monday's, but don't know anything against him in reference to this business.

MR. MARTIN stated that Denbow bore a good character.

THE COURT unanimously found Denbow guilty, and passed upon him the following sentence: That he be imprisoned in the Work House of Charleston until his master, under the direction of the City Council of Charleston, shall send him out of the limits of the United States, into which he is not to return under the penalty of death.

UPON GEORGE, BILLY, PEIRAULT, FRANK, AND JOHN, who had pleaded guilty, and had been used as witnesses, the Court passed the following sentence: That they be imprisoned in the Work House of Charleston until their masters, under the direction of the City Council of Charleston shall send them out of the limits of the United States, into which they are not to return under penalty of death.

EXAMINATION OF BILLY, taken a day or two after his arrest —The first meeting was at Mr. Thayer's farm—one Sunday morning I joined them there, but did not learn what was done there, and I left them. After that, they came to Mr. Bulkley's farm—this was in April. At that meeting there were Adam Robertson, Robert Robertson, John Robertson, Dick Simms, and Polydore Faber. At that meeting they were consulting about the means of rising against the whites. Gullah Jack was present, he came in company with Adam and Robert—they roasted a fowl, and ate it half raw, as an evidence of union. Robert and Gullah Jack were the principal men. One day I met Adam, on my return from market, and he requested me to hide a jug of powder, and I refused to do so. At another meeting, before the 16th June, at which the following persons were present, viz: Adam, Robert, Polydore, John Robertson, Dick Simms, and Gullah Jack. A pistol was exhibited, and everyone tried to fire it, but no one could discharge it, but Dick Simms. Those, in whose hands it could not go off, were considered as safe. Charles Drayton told me, that the place of meeting for the draymen was to be the farm of Mr. Payne—and Charles also informed me, that they wished to put their horses in my master's farm, which I refused. Charles afterwards told me that the plot was discovered, and that the blacks must remain quiet, until the whites were off their guard. Robert called and gave me the same caution that Adam had done. Peter Poyas and others, whom I know not, came to the farm, on the night of the 27th of April, about 8 P.M. and sang and prayed until daylight. Before this time, I asked Robert who was the principal man, he said Gullah Jack. I then asked him, if there were no others; he said that Gullah Jack had gone to Father Morris, (Morris Brown) to ask him whether he would sanction the insurrection, and Morris Brown replied, if you can get men go on, but don't mention my name. I am going shortly to the North and I shall hear there, what you are about.

Will Bee told Peter Ward, who mentioned it to me, that all the draymen, without exception, would be light-horsemen. Polydore belonging to Mrs. Faber, hid more than twenty poles, about 10 feet long, on Mr. Bulkley's farm, under the house. Polydore said that Robert would come, and I supposed that he was coming to fix something at the end of the poles. Robert came in the afternoon and said that it was useless, as the business was discovered.

There was a number of other persons charged with the same offence and arraigned by the Court, but the evidence against them being thought insufficient they were discharged without being put upon their trials.

On Friday the 25th July the Court adjourned, *sine die,* having disposed of every case before them after a session of nearly six weeks.

The following account of the Trials before the second Court was politely furnished by one of its Members: In Consequence of the Dissolution of the Court over which Lionel H. Kennedy and Thomas Parker, Esq'rs., Presided, a new Court was organized for the trial of William Garner, who had recently been apprehended in Columbia, and brought to Charleston, and of such other slaves as might be brought before them.

THE COURT met accordingly, and consisted of the following Gentlemen, viz:

JACOB AXSON, Q. U.	⎫ *Magistrates.*
CHARLES M. FURMAN, J. P.	⎭
THOS. RHETT SMITH,	⎫
JOEL R. POINSETT,	⎪
ROBERT Y. HAYNE,	⎬ *Freeholders.*
THOMAS ROPER,	⎪
JOHN GORDON,	⎭

After a free interchange of sentiments, the members of this Court were unanimously of the opinion, that with respect to capital punishments, enough had been done by way of example in relation to this conspiracy, and that where the Court might feel themselves compelled by the weight of the evidence to convict, they would punish the offenders by banishment, and that they would only inflict capital punishment where the criminal should appear to have been a leader, or where his case was distinguished by very peculiar circumstances. Fourteen persons were tried by this Court —of these six were acquitted, and eight found guilty—of the latter, seven were sentenced to transportation beyond the limits of the United States, and one (William Garner) was sentenced to death and suffered accordingly. The case of William Garner was one which, in the unanimous opinion of the Court came within the rule established by them. It was fully proved that he *was a leader,* on whom much reliance was placed; he was to have headed a party of the horse, and agreed to enlist men for that service among the draymen. He stated to the witness that he had made some progress in that service, and when his fears were excited on account of the detection of the conspiracy, he did not seem disposed to abandon the enterprise, though he offered to give up to another his command in the horse. It was fully proved that Garner had entered heartily into the scheme, and was very earnest in his inquiries about the extent of the preparations. The Court having resolved to put no questions to any of the prisoners which might induce them to criminate themselves, of course did not question Garner, but on the evidence against him being closed, and on his counsel declaring that he had nothing to urge in his defence, the prisoner requested that he might be permitted to speak for himself. This being granted, he spoke with great fluency for nearly half an hour, and made a defence, which for ingenuity, would have done honor to an educated man. Finding that *four witnesses, separately examined,* had concurred in establishing facts which must lead irresistibly to his conviction, he boldly admitted the whole of the facts stated in evidence, and alleged that his intention from the beginning had been to possess himself of full information concerning the details of the plot—to discover the deposit of arms and ammunition, and then to betray the conspirators to the white people. He stated that the premature discovery of the plot had alone prevented him from executing this purpose, and finally made an appeal to the Court, and asked "whether a man situated as he was—master of his own time, as good as free (and as he emphatically expressed it) 'as happy as the days were long,' could have any motive to engage in such a scheme." The Court could not give credit to these *secret intentions* of the prisoner, contradicted as they were by his acts; especially as it would have been so easy for him to have given *private information* to some white person, and thus have put his intentions beyond a doubt. The circumstance of his having fled from Charleston also weighed against him; and though he had a ticket from his indulgent mistress, the Court were not on that account the less convinced that Garner's journey to Columbia was undertaken by him as the means of escaping from punishment. His being detected and brought back to Charleston was certainly calculated to make a deep impression on the minds of the slaves. In every view of the subject, therefore Garner's case seemed to demand the utmost penalty of the law, and it was inflicted accordingly.

In the progress of the trials before this Court one or two circumstances occurred worthy of being noticed. The Court at the commencement of their investigations determined thoroughly to examine into the degree of credit to be attached to the witnesses, and were very particular in their inquiries in respect to the two principal witnesses, Monday Gell and Peirault. It appeared that the character of these men for veracity and honesty, had been unexceptional through life. Monday indeed seemed to have been distinguished for the candor, sobriety, and integrity of his life, and of Peirault, his master declared that his only fault was "that he was sometimes so blunt and free spoken, as to approach to rudeness." The Court were finally of the opinion that entire reliance could be placed on these two witnesses, and that every word which came from Monday could be implicitly relied on. Several circumstances occurred during the trials to confirm the favorable impressions of the Court with respect to these witnesses —one or two of them will be here stated. The witnesses were not permitted to have any communications with each other, and they were never informed of the particular prisoner against whom they were to appear. They were brought forth separately and examined. Their *concurrence,* under such circumstances, certainly afforded strong evidence of their truth. On Monday Gell's detailed conversation he had with Michaw (and which was favorable to the prisoner). Mr. Miller, who was present, stated promptly to the Court that Michaw himself had stated to him the same conversation, in all particulars, as soon as he was arrested; and it appeared that no communication had since taken place between the parties. Of several similar circumstances, only one other will be here noticed. It appeared that Garner, Monday, Peter Poyas, and others, had held a meeting at the house of a blind man named Philip. Monday stated in his evidence before the Court, concerning that meeting, that this man addressed Garner, and asked him, "why he looked so timorous," and quoted a text of Scripture, "Why should thy heart be troubled? . . ." It appeared so extraordinary, that a blind man should speak of another's *looks,* that some suspicion rested on Monday's statement. The blind man was sent for, and on being brought forward (though totally ignorant of the statements made by Monday) stated the remark he had made to Garner about "his timorous looks." Garner in his defence, admitted that this remark had been made and said it had greatly alarmed him at the time, knowing that the old man was blind.[25]

Two cases were brought before this Court, which furnished

incidents worthy of remark. In one of them it was proved that
Vesey had forbidden his followers to trust the prisoner, "because
on one occasion he had been seen in a state of intoxication." In
the other case, that of George (slave of Samuel Parker), it appeared that Vesey, Monday Gell, and the other leaders of the
conspiracy came to a resolution that the prisoner should not be
trusted. He was an African, but they alleged against him, that he
did not associate with his countrymen, and was a babbling fellow,
on whom no dependence could be placed. George had heard something about an insurrection, and resolved to have his hand in it.
He went about among the conspirators, declared himself one of
them, and both by actions and words, manifested a determination
to take his part in the contest. He was (notwithstanding his un-
questionable good will to the cause) uniformly rejected as a
Marplot who could not be trusted. When brought before the Court
the levity of manner which distinguished this Negro, convinced
the Court of the wisdom and circumspection displayed by the
leaders of the conspiracy in excluding him from their ranks.

The three following sentences were pronounced by Lionel H.
Kennedy, Esquire, the presiding Magistrate of the first Court,
organized for the trial of slaves and other persons of color,
charged with attempting to raise an insurrection in this State.
Several other sentences were delivered, but were not reduced into
writing.

SENTENCE ON DENMARK VESEY, a free black man—
Denmark Vesey: the Court, on mature consideration, have pronounced you guilty. You have enjoyed the advantage of able
Counsel, and were also heard in your own defence, in which you
endeavored, with great art and plausibility, to impress a belief of
your innocence. After the most patient deliberation, however, the
Court were not only satisfied of your guilt, but that you were the
author and original instigator of this diabolical plot. Your professed design was to trample on all laws, human and divine; to
riot in blood, outrage, rapine, and conflagration, and to introduce
anarchy and confusion in their most horrid forms. Your life has
become, therefore, a just and necessary sacrifice, at the shrine of
indignant justice. It is difficult to imagine what *infatuation* could

have prompted you to attempt an enterprise so wild and visionary. You were a free man; were comparatively wealthy; and enjoyed every comfort compatible with your situation. You had, therefore, much to risk, and little to gain. From your age and experience, you *ought* to have known, that success was impracticable.

A moment's reflection must have convinced you, that the ruin of *your race,* would have been the probable result, and that years would have rolled away, before they could have recovered that confidence which they once enjoyed in this community. The only reparation in your power is a full disclosure of the truth. In addition to treason, you have committed the grossest impiety, in attempting to pervert the sacred words of God into a sanction for crimes of the blackest hue. It is evident, that you are totally insensible of the divine influence of that Gospel, "all whose paths are peace." It was to reconcile us to our destinies on earth, and to enable us to discharge with fidelity, all the duties of life, that those holy precepts were imparted by Heaven to fallen man.

If you had searched them with sincerity, you would have discovered instructions, immediately applicable to the deluded victims of your artful wiles—"Servants (says Saint Paul) obey in all things your masters, according to the flesh, not with eye-service, as menpleasers, but in singleness of heart, fearing God." And again "Servants (says Saint Peter) be subject to your masters with all fear, not only to the good and gentle, but also to the froward." On such texts comment is unnecessary.

Your "lamp of life" is nearly extinguished; your race is run, and you must shortly pass "from time to eternity." Let me then conjure you to devote the remnant of your existence in solemn preparation for the awful doom that awaits you. Your situation is deplorable, but not destitute of spiritual consolation. To that Almighty Being alone, whose Holy Ordinances you have trampled in the dust, can you now look for mercy, and although "your sins be as scarlet," the tears of sincere penitence may obtain forgiveness at the "Throne of Grace." You cannot have forgotten the history of the malefactor on the Cross, who, like yourself, was the wretched and deluded victim of offended justice. His conscience was awakened in the pangs of dissolution, and yet there is reason to believe, that his spirit was received into the realms of bliss.

May *you* imitate his example, and may *your* last moments prove like his!

SENTENCE ON JACK, a slave belonging to Paul Pritchard, commonly called Gullah Jack, and sometimes Cooter Jack—Gullah Jack: the Court after deliberately considering all the circumstances of your case, are perfectly satisfied of your guilt. In the prosecution of your wicked designs, you were not satisfied with resorting to natural and ordinary means, but endeavored to enlist on your behalf, all the powers of darkness, and employed for that purpose, the most disgusting mummery and superstition. You represented yourself as invulnerable; that you could neither be taken nor destroyed, and that all who fought under your banners would be invincible. While such wretched expedients are calculated to excite the confidence, or to alarm the fears of the ignorant and credulous, they produce no other emotion in the minds of the intelligent and enlightened, but contempt and disgust. Your boasted charms have not preserved yourself, and of course could not protect others. Your altars and your Gods have sunk together in the dust. The airy spectres, conjured by you, have been chased away by the superior light of Truth, and you stand exposed, the miserable and deluded victim of offended justice. Your days are literally numbered. You will shortly be consigned to the cold and silent grave; and all the Powers of Darkness cannot rescue you from your approaching Fate! Let me then, conjure you to devote the remnant of your miserable existence, in fleeing from the *wrath to come.* This can only be done by a full disclosure of the truth. The Court are willing to afford you all the aid in their power, and to permit any Minister of the Gospel, whom you may select to have free access to you. To him you may unburden your guilty conscience. Neglect not the opportunity, for there is no device nor art in the grave, to which you must shortly be consigned.

SENTENCE OF TEN OF THE CRIMINALS—the Court, on mature deliberation, have pronounced you guilty; the punishment of that guilt is death. Your conduct, on the present occasion, exhibits a degree of depravity and extravagance, rarely paralleled. Your professed objects were to trample not only on the laws of this state, but on those of humanity; to commit murder, outrage, and plunder, and to substitute for the blessings we enjoy, anarchy and confusion in their most odious forms. The beauties of nature and of art, would have fallen victims to your relentless fury; and even the decrepitude of age and the innocence of childhood, would have found no other refuge than the grave!

Surely nothing but infatuation could have prompted you to enter into a plot so wild and diabolical. A moment's reflection would have convinced you, that disgrace and ruin must have been its consequence, and that it would have probably resulted in the destruction and extermination of *your race*. But if, even complete success had crowned your efforts, what were the golden visions which you anticipated? Such men as you, are in general as ignorant as you are vicious, without any settled principles, and possessing but few of the virtues of civilized life; you would soon, therefore, have degenerated into a horde of barbarians, incapable of any government. But admitting that a different result might have taken place, it is natural to inquire, what are the miseries of which you complain? That we should all earn our bread by the sweat of our brow, is the decree which God pronounced at the fall of man. It extended alike to the master and the slave; to the cottage and the throne. Everyone is more or less subject to control; and the most exalted, as well as the humblest individual, must bow with deference to the laws of that community, in which he is placed by Providence. Your situation, therefore, was neither extraordinary nor unnatural. Servitude has existed under various forms, from the deluge to the present time, and in no age or country has the condition of slaves been milder or more humane than your own. You are, with few exceptions, treated with kindness, and enjoy every comfort compatible with your situation. You are exempt from many of the miseries, to which *the poor* are subject throughout the world. In many countries the life of the slave is at the disposal of his master; here you have always been under the protection of the law.

The tribunal which now imposes this sentence through its humble organ, affords a strong exemplification of the truth of these remarks. In the discharge of the painful duties which have devolved on them the members of this Court have been as anxious to acquit the innocent as determined to condemn the guilty.

In addition to the crime of treason, you have on the present occasion, displayed the vilest ingratitude. It is a melancholy truth, that those servants in whom was reposed the most unlimited confidence, have been the principal actors in this wicked scheme. Reared by the hand of kindness, and fostered by a master who assumed many of the duties of a parent—you have realized the fable of the Frozen Serpent, and attempted to destroy the bosom that sheltered and protected you.

You have moreover committed the grossest impiety: you have perverted the sacred words of God, and attempted to torture them into a sanction for crimes, at the bare imagination of which, humanity shudders. Are you incapable of the Heavenly influence of that Gospel, all whose "paths are peace"? It was to reconcile us to our destiny on earth, and to enable us to discharge with fidelity all our duties, whether as master or servant, that those inspired precepts were imparted by Heaven to fallen man. There is no condition of life which is not embraced by them; and if you had searched them, *in the spirit of truth,* you would have discovered instructions peculiarly applicable to yourselves—*Servants (says St. Paul) be obedient to them that are your masters according to the flesh, with fear and trembling, in singleness of your heart, as unto Christ; not with eye-service as menpleasers, but as the servants of Christ, doing the will of God from the heart.* Had you listened with sincerity to such doctrines, you would not have been arrested by an ignominious death.

Your days on earth are near their close and you now stand upon the confines of eternity. While you linger on this side of the grave, permit me to exhort you, in the name of the everliving God, whose holy ordinances you have violated; to devote most earnestly the remnant of your days, in penitence and preparation for that tribunal, whose sentence, whether pronounced in anger or in mercy, is eternal.

The following were the Negroes on whom the above sentence was pronounced: Dick, Bacchus, William, Naphur, Adam, Bellisle, Charles, Jemmy, Jerry, and Dean.

A CALENDAR comprising those arrested, their owner's names, the time of their commitment, and the manner in which they were disposed of.

CLASS NO. 1.

Comprises those prisoners who were found guilty and executed.

PRISONERS	OWNERS	TIME OF COMMIT.	HOW DISPOSED OF
Peter	James Poyas	June 18	Hanged on Tuesday the 2d July, 1822, on Blake's lands, near Charleston.
Ned	Gov. T. Bennett	*ditto*	
Rolla	*ditto*	*ditto*	
Batteau	*ditto*	*ditto*	
Denmark Vesey	A free black man	22	
Jesse	Thos. Blackwood	23	
John	Elias Horry	July 5	*Ditto* on the lines near Charleston; Friday, July 12.
Gullah Jack	Paul Pritchard	*ditto*	
Mingo	Wm. Harth	June 21	Hanged on the lines near Charleston, on Friday, 26th, July.
Lot	Forrester	24	
Joe	P. L. Jore	July 6	
Julius	Thos. Forrest	8	
Tom	Mrs. Russel	10	
Smart	Rob't. Anderson	*ditto*	
John	John Robertson	11	
Robert	*ditto*	*ditto*	
Adam	*ditto*	*ditto*	
Polydore	Mrs. Faber	*ditto*	
Bacchus	Benj. Hammet	*ditto*	
Dick	Wm. Simms	13	
Pharo	Mrs. Thompson	*ditto*	
Jemmy	Mrs. Clement	18	
Jerry	Mordecai Cohen	19	
Dean	Jas. Mitchell	*ditto*	
Jack	Mrs. Purcell	12	
Bellisle	Est. of Jos. Yates	18	
Naphur	*ditto*	*ditto*	
Adam	*ditto*	*ditto*	
Jack	John S. Glenn	16	
Charles	John Billings	18	

Jack	N. McNeil	22	
Caesar	Miss Smith	*ditto*	*Ditto* Tuesday, July
Jacob Stagg	Jacob Lancaster	23	30.
Tom	Wm. M. Scott	24	
[26] William	Mrs. Garner	Aug. 2	*Ditto* Friday, Aug. 9.

CLASS NO. 2.

Comprises those prisoners who were found guilty, and sentenced to death, but recommended by the Court of Magistrates and free-holders, to the Governor to be pardoned upon condition that they be sent out of the limits of the United States.

They were respited to the 25th day of October, 1822, with a view to the commutation of their punishment to banishment beyond the limits of the United States; but since the respite, the Governor has pardoned Peter Cooper, upon condition of his receiving twenty lashes.

PRISONERS	OWNERS	TIME OF COMMIT.	HOW DISPOSED OF
Louis	Cromwell	July 1	
Seymour	Kunhardt	*ditto*	Respited until the
Saby Gaillard	A free black man	13	25th of October;
Isaac	Wm. Harth	*ditto*	and now confined
Paris	Mrs. Ball	16	in the Work
Peter	Mrs. Cooper	*ditto*	House of Charles-
Dublin	C. G. Morris	18	ton.
George	Thos. Bampfield	*ditto*	
Sandy	Jacob Schnell	19	

CLASS NO. 3.

Comprises those prisoners who were found guilty and sentenced to death, but since respited by the Executive, until the 25th of Oct. with a view to the commutation of their punishment, to banishment beyond the limits of the United States.

PRISONERS	OWNERS	TIME OF COMMIT.	HOW DISPOSED OF
William	Job Palmer	July 18	Respited till Oct.
John Vincent	D. Cruckshanks	23	25, and is now in
Billy Robinson	P. Robinson	*ditto*	the Work House.

CLASS NO. 4.

Comprises those prisoners who were found guilty and sentenced to be transported, beyond the limits of the United States, by their masters, under the direction of the City Council.

PRISONERS	OWNERS	TIME OF COMMIT.	HOW DISPOSED OF
Monday	John Gell	June 27	Confined in the Work House & sen. to death com. to ban. out U.S.
Charles	Hon. J. Drayton	July 2	
Harry	David Haig	3	
Frank	Mrs. Ferguson	June 27	
George	Mr. Vanderhorst	July 6	
Peirault	Strohecker	10	
Billy	S. Bulkley	*ditto*	
John	Mr. Enslow	13	
Scipio	Wm. Sims	*ditto*	
Agrippa	Mrs. Perry	19	
27 Pompey	Rich. Lord	Aug. 5	Confined in the Work House.
Sam	Mr. Barnstile	*ditto*	
Dembo	J. N. Martin	25	
27 Nero	David Haig	Aug. 3	
27 Jack	Wm. Cattell	5	
27 George	Mr. Evans	6	
27 Harry	Mr. Butler	*ditto*	
27 George	Sam. Parker	*ditto*	
27 Adam Bellamy	J. H. Merritt	3	

CLASS NO. 5.

Comprises those who were found guilty and sentenced to be transported beyond the limits of the State of South Carolina.

PRISONER	OWNER	TIME OF COMMIT.	HOW DISPOSED OF
Prince Graham	A free black man	July 21	Sentenced to be imprisoned one month in the Work House, and then transported beyond the limits of the State.

CLASS NO. 6.

Comprises those prisoners who were acquitted by the Court, their guilt not being fully proved. The Court, however, have suggested to their owners, the propriety of transporting them beyond the limits of the United States.

PRISONERS	OWNERS	TIME OF COMMIT.	HOW DISPOSED OF
Buonaparte	Francis Mulligan	July 11	Acquitted by Court, master advised to transport, and now in the Work House, Charleston.
Abraham	Dr. Poyas	June 22	
Butcher	James L. Gibbs	July 11	
John	Mrs. Taylor	13	
Prince	Miss Righton	19	
Edwin	Mr. J. Paul	24	
Quash Harleston	A free black man	July 29	—By arrangement with Counsel, gone out of the U.S.
Harry Purse	Wm. Purse	not arrested	Arranged with owners to be transported.
Panza	Mr. Mitchell		
Liverpool	Mrs. Hunt		
William	John Paul	Mar. 31	Confined in the Work House under an arrangement by Counsel with his master to be transported.

CLASS NO. 7.

Comprises those prisoners who were acquitted by the Courts of Magistrates and freeholders, and discharged.

PRISONERS	OWNERS	TIME OF COMMIT.	HOW DISPOSED OF
Stephen	T. Rhett Smith	June 18	
Amherst	Mrs. Lining	*ditto*	
Saml. Guifford	A free black lad	20	
Robt. Hadden	A free mul. boy	*ditto*	
Friday	Mr. Rout	23	
Jeffry Grant	A free black man	20	
Jim	J. H. Ancrum	22	Acquitted
William	Mrs. Colcock	July 12	and
Pierre Louis	Mons. Chappeau	*ditto* 18	Discharged
[28] Pompey	David Haig	June 23	
[28] Philander	A free col. man	Aug. 8	
[28] Edw'd Johnson	A free black man	*ditto*	
[28] Stephen Walker	Mr. Walker	*ditto* 5	
[28] James	*ditto*	*ditto*	
[28] Harry	J. Nell	*ditto* 6	

CLASS NO. 8.

Comprises those persons who were discharged after being arrested, the testimony against them not being sufficient to bring them to trial.

PRISONERS	OWNERS	TIME OF COMMIT.
Mathias	Thos. Bennett	June 18
Mungo	James Poyas	*ditto*
Bram	Jonathan Lucas	20
Richard	*ditto*	17
John	*ditto*	*ditto*
Hercules	Mr. Clark	20
Sandy	H. P. Holmes	25
Lemon	Mr. Houston	23
Adam	Mrs. Ferguson	27

PRISONERS	OWNERS	TIME OF COMMIT.	
Pompey	John Bryan		28
Harry	Mr. Harleston		
Robert Nesbitt	A Free Man	July	3
Patrick	Miss Datty		4
Thomas	S. Magwood		5
Charles	F. G. Deliesseline		8
William	Mr. Adger		10
Smart	Mrs. Ward		*ditto*
Peter	*ditto*		*ditto*
Sandy	Francis Curtis		11
Isaac	Paul Trapier		*ditto*
Charles	Mrs. Shubrick		*ditto*
Cuffy	Charles Graves		*ditto*
Mungo	Wm. Lowndes		*ditto*
Thomas	A. Lord		*ditto*
Bob	Mr. Hibben		13
Albert	T. Inglis, a free mulatto man.		15
Jim	Mr. Happoldt		*ditto*
John	Mr. Gates		*ditto*
Charles	Mr. Hasell		*ditto*
James	Mr. Dowling		17
Prince	*ditto*		*ditto*
Caesar	Mrs. Parker		19
Billy	Mr. Fordham		20
Ben	Mr. Cammer		22
William	Mr. Cromwell		*ditto*
Stephen	Mr. Harper		26
Louis	John Gell		18
Pompey	John Bryan	Aug.	5

RECAPITULATION.

Number of prisoners	executed—See Class No. 1.	35
"	" respited with a view to their transportation—see Classes Nos. 2 and 3.	12
"	" sentenced to be transported by their owners, under the direction of the City Council *beyond the limits of the United States*—see Class, No. 4.	19
"	" sentenced to be transported out of the State—see Class, No. 5.	1
"	" acquitted, but suggested to owners to transport—see Class, No. 6	11
"	" acquitted—see Class No. 7.	15
"	" discharged—see Class, No. 8.	38
Whole number arrested,		131

APPENDIX

At a Court of Sessions held at Charleston, on the 7th October, 1822, before his honor Judge Bay, four men were tried and convicted of a Misdemeanor in inciting Slaves to insurrection.

These cases created much interest, in consequence of their connection with the late attempt made by the slaves, to raise an insurrection in this state. It did not appear that the prisoners were actually concerned in the insurrection, any further than in exciting the slaves. The plot certainly did not originate with white persons, nor was it ever communicated by any person concerned in it, to a single white man, until the information was given which led to the development of the scheme.

It has appeared, however, that as soon as rumors of a Negro plot went abroad, some white men of the lowest characters, determined to avail themselves of the occasion, and by exciting the slaves hasten an event, which however calamitous to the rest of the community, they vainly imagined might be beneficial to themselves. Whether any of these men would actually have taken part with the slaves in the conduct of the insurrection, and whether the slaves themselves would have permitted white men to act in their ranks cannot be now ascertained. It is presumed that plunder, and indemnity to their own persons, were the objects sought for by these offenders. Only four individuals have been detected and brought to punishment for the crime of "inciting slaves to insurrection." Against these, the testimony of white persons was obtained; but when the nature of the crime, the secrecy that would naturally have been observed, and the incompetency of slaves to give evidence, are duly considered, there is every reason to believe that many other cases (perhaps more aggravated) have existed, and which still remain undiscovered. It cannot be doubted, that there are to be found in the city of Charleston, desperate men, (outcasts from countries from which they have been banished for crimes,) who hold themselves in readiness at a moment's warning, to engage in any enterprise of blood and ruin, from which plunder may be gained. It will be the part of wisdom to mark and profit by, every fact and circumstance connected with the late conspiracy. The indictment and conviction of the persons hereinafter named, is an incident in the late transactions in this city, too important to be overlooked; a brief report of their cases is therefore annexed.

THE STATE OF SOUTH CAROLINA, vs. WILLIAM ALLEN. —*Indictment for a Misdemeanor, in inciting slaves to insurrection.* This was a tall, stout, fine looking sailor, a Scotchman by birth, about forty-five years of age, and who had recently arrived in Charleston. It appeared that having fallen in company with a free man of color, named *Scott,* at the time when the city was much agitated by the rumors of the late intended insurrection, he inquired of Scott concerning it; and not only urged the execution of the plan, but stated his willingness to be concerned in it. Scott immediately gave this information to John Stoney, Esq., an eminent merchant of this city, who directed him to assume an apparent willingness to engage in the plot, and see to what extent Allen would go. In order to identify the man, Scott led him into the store of William E. Snowden, Esq., on the pretence of business. Several interviews took place between Scott and Allen, and it was finally agreed between them, that they should meet at night, at the house of a free Negro man named Joe, the father-in-law of Scott, where the subject was to be fully considered. Hitherto the evidence against Allen was not such as could have led to his conviction; but arrangements were now made to obtain full information, and decisive evidence of the nature and extent of his guilt. Information having been given to his Honor James Hamilton, Jr., Intendant of the City of Charleston, of the contemplated meeting, he summoned Richard W. Cogdell, Esq., one of the wardens, to his assistance, and they repaired to the house of the Negro Joe.

They concealed themselves in a small upper room, which was so dark that they could distinctly see and hear everything which passed below, without themselves being observed. Soon after, Allen entered with Scott, and was introduced to Joe. No other persons were present in the room below. As soon as Allen entered the room, he expressed apprehensions that he might be overheard—examined the room, and asked that the windows and doors be carefully closed. He stated also, that he was armed, and threatened vengeance if betrayed. The Negroes soon succeeded, however, in removing his apprehensions—some brandy was produced, and the three sat down together at a table, and entered upon the business of the meeting. During a conversation which lasted nearly two hours, Allen expressed his approbation of the scheme of attempting an insurrection—urged the usual arguments in justification of such a measure, and explicitly declared that he would take part in it. He furnished ready answers to every objection that was urged, and endeavored to remove all the difficulties that were suggested. In doing this, he certainly made false statements, intended, however, to give confidence to the blacks. He pretended, for instance, to be acquainted with the plans, and spoke of large parcels of arms secreted near the city. In speaking of the plan of operations, he declared "that it would take 400 men to make the grand stand," and added, "that he would head them as soon as that number was obtained." He added, however, that he knew a Captain of a vessel, whom he named, (who then resided in Elliott Street) who had been a pirate for 15 years, and was in all respects qualified to be the leader of the expedition.[29] He insisted that this man should be obtained, and that he (Allen) would serve under him. He spoke freely of the operations, and declared it to be his opinion, *that there ought to be an indiscriminate destruction of all the whites, men, women and children*. In the course of the interview, the Negroes objected that he (Allen) being a white man, could not be safely trusted by them. To this he replied, that "though he had a white face, he was a Negro in heart." As the party below continued to drink, Allen, before the end of the interview, became somewhat intoxicated, though he had been sober at the commencement. The Intendant and Mr. Cogdell, from their place of concealment, had a distinct view of everything which was passing in the room below, and expecting opposition, and finding that Allen was a strong, stout man, and probably armed, they made their arrangements for overcoming him. Allen finally rose to depart, and being immediately followed by the gentlemen above mentioned, was seized in the street by them, and taken to the Guard House. He made no resistance, and seemed so completely subdued by his fears, that no doubt could be entertained that he was by no means qualified on the score of courage, to conduct a dangerous enterprise. In the course of the interview, Allen explicitly declared, that he looked for a handsome pecuniary reward for the services he was to render, and hinted that the freedom of the blacks was an object of no importance to him.

From this circumstance, and his making false statements in relation to the arms, and pretending that he was one of the initiated, it is clear that Allen was not actually engaged in the conspiracy; that his object was money, and that he would probably have been content in urging the ignorant blacks to an attempt, which in any event, must have produced the most lamentable consequences. At his trial, Allen made no defence, though his ingenious counsel urged some points of law to the court, as to the legal character of the offence. The Jury found him guilty without hesitation. He was sentenced to be imprisoned twelve months; to pay a fine of one thousand dollars, and to find security for his good behavior for five years after his liberation. This sentence, unless modified by a pardon, will doubtless amount to imprisonment for life, since the circumstances and character of the prisoner, will effectually prevent him from paying the fine, or giving the security. After the sentence was passed, Allen addressed the Court in a clear, distinct voice, and with considerable ingenuity. He gave a brief history of his life, and stated that he had served on board of two American privateers during the late war, and also in the navy of the United States—that he had been in several severe actions, and was a pensioner of war in England. His strong Scottish dialect, however, might lead us to doubt his having been so long in this country. Certain it is, that he had never been a resident in Charleston, and had very recently arrived here before the disclosure of the late insurrectionary movements.

THE STATE, vs. JOHN IGNESHIAS.—This man was indicted for the same offence.

He is a Spaniard, a seafaring man, about forty or forty-five years of age, tall, very athletic, and of a steady determined countenance. He speaks broken English, but so as to be easily understood. The evidence against him was, that he was overheard (by Mr. Joseph Hill, and his sister, Mrs. Silvea,) in conversation with a slave, supposed to be the property of Mr. Lance. There were several other Negroes, however, (fishermen) present. In this conversation, (part of which was overheard by the witnesses,) the prisoner began by declaring that "he disliked everything in Charleston, but the Negroes and the sailors." The slave replied, "that he liked everyone who used him well." The prisoner then remarked, "how can you think the white people use you well by keeping you in slavery?" and added, "If you had a favor to ask, would you ask it of a white man or a black man, and will any white man trust you for anything?" The Negro, whose fidelity was not to be shaken, replied, "that he had received many favors from the white people, that they were his best friends," and then specified some instances, particularly one of his having recently bought some articles on credit. The patience of the Spaniard was now completely exhausted, and he exclaimed with anger, "damn them, I would kill them all," alluding, as the witness explained it, to what the Negroes ought to do towards the whites.

On this evidence the prisoner was found guilty of inciting slaves to insurrection, and was sentenced to three months imprisonment, to pay a fine of $100, and to give security for good behavior for five years.

The prisoner at his trial, and on receiving sentence, addressed the Court, and insisted that the witnesses were mistaken as to his identity, and claimed for himself the character of an honest and industrious man.

THE STATE vs. JACOB DANDERS.—This man was indicted for the same offence.

He is a German, of low stature, and apparently of dissipated habits; about forty-five or fifty years of age. The charge against him was, that he was heard by a most respectable witness (Mr.

Joseph Young,) speaking to several Negroes concerning the execution of some of the slaves. "Poor creatures," said he, "my heart bleeds for you; the Negroes executed were innocent, and have been all murdered, and you (addressing himself to the Negroes), ought not to have permitted it, and you must rescue those who are still to be hanged," and added, "that he was himself a Lawyer and a Preacher."

On this evidence the prisoner was found guilty. The prisoner addressed the Court very fluently in broken German. He did not attempt to deny having spoken the words attributed to him, but said he was intoxicated at the time. Mr. Young, however, declared, that he might have been a little intoxicated, but knew perfectly well what he was about. Danders had been but a short time in Charleston; had been engaged as a pedlar, selling trifling articles, and in his course of life was very much of a vagabond. He was sentenced to three months imprisonment, to pay a fine of $100, and to give security for his good behavior for five years.

THE STATE, vs. ANDREW S. RHODES.—
This was a tall, fine looking portly man, about fifty years of age, with a fresh complexion, and wearing a light colored wig. He was well known in Charleston, having been a few Courts ago convicted of swindling Mr. Foster Burnet, of this city, by means of a counterfeit letter. The prisoner did not state where he was born and brought up, but said that he had been thirty years in this State, a part of which time he kept a small shop in one of the country parishes in the neighborhood of Charleston.

The testimony against Rhodes was certainly less satisfactory than against either of the other prisoners. A woman by the name of Mary Shively stated that Rhodes came to the house of Adam Garden (a free man of color,) from whom the witness hires a room, and there in the presence of Garden, and of two other men of color who were present, commenced speaking of Gullah Jack, who had been sentenced to be hanged. The prisoner, speaking of that event, introduced the name of a respectable gentleman, and said he ought to be hanged in the place of Gullah Jack, and then added, "the Negroes ought to fight for their liberty . . . that they had as much right to fight for their liberty as the white people." He stated, "that he would head them in the enterprise, and that in three weeks he would have 2,000 men."

The witness here added, that Rhodes then said that "all the white women would soon have black husbands." The three colored men gave no encouragement to the prisoner, and seemed very much frightened. The witness reproached the prisoner with holding such language, and he became very abusive. The free persons of color not being admissible witnesses, were, of course, not examined. Two of the circumstances stated by Mary Shively, were not found in her affidavit before the Magistrates, viz: the statement about the 2,000 men and the women having Negro husbands. The ingenious counsel for the prisoner, endeavored on this ground, to discredit the witness, and also submitted some points of law in defence of the prisoner. The Jury however, found him guilty, and he was sentenced to six months imprisonment, to pay a fine of $500, and to find security for his good behavior, for five years. After receiving his sentence, Rhodes addressed the Court in a very clear and ingenious speech, protesting his innocence, and insisting that his whole life had been one of innocence and good conduct, notwithstanding which, he had constantly suffered oppression and injustice.

It is certainly worthy of remark, that none of the slaves or free persons of color assailed by the seditious language of the prisoners, manifested any disposition to engage in the conspiracy. Scott immediately gave information to Mr. Stoney. Mr. Lance's slave not only combatted the arguments of Igneshias, but acknowledged his obligations to the white people. None of the Negroes to whom Danders addressed himself, gave him the least encouragement, and it was proved that Rhodes' auditors displayed great alarm. These degenerate white men, perhaps, fell in with faithful servants who were not to be seduced into crimes; or the proposition, coming from white men, excited suspicion and distrust; or what is still more probable, the punishments recently inflicted on the conspirators, had excited a salutary alarm.

[*Note.* The Attorney General indicted these men for Misdemeanor at common law, being of opinion that their cases were not embraced within the letter of the Act of Assembly of 1805, which inflicts capital punishment on persons connected with slaves in actual insurrection. The Act is in these words, viz. "Be it enacted, that from and immediately after the passing of this Act, every person or persons, who shall, or may be, either directly or indirectly, concerned or connected with any slave or slaves, in a state of actual insurrection within this state; or who shall, in any manner or to any extent, excite, counsel, advise, induce, aid, comfort, or assist any slave or slaves to raise, or attempt to raise an insurrection within this state, by furnishing them with any written or other passport, with any arms or ammunition, or munition of war; or knowing of their assembling for any purpose tending to treason or insurrection, shall afford to them shelter or protection, or shall permit his, her, or their house, or houses, to be resorted to by any slave or slaves, for any purpose tending to treason or insurrection, as aforesaid, shall on conviction thereof in any Court having jurisdiction thereof, by confession in open Court, or by the testimony of two witnesses, be adjudged guilty of treason against the state, and suffer death."

On this Act it must be observed that the first clause punishes with death white persons who shall be concerned with slaves in actual insurrection. All the slaves who have been convicted, were found guilty merely of "an attempt to raise an insurrection;" and it was never pretended that any actual insurrection existed. The remaining clauses of the act provide for the punishment of offenders who shall aid and assist slaves in raising an insurrection, by one of the following means, viz.

1. By furnishing them with passports.

2. By furnishing them with arms or munitions of war.

3. By affording them shelter and protection when knowing of their assembling for any purpose tending to treason.

4. By permitting his or their house to be resorted to by slaves, for any purpose tending to treason.

In the cases reported, none of these specific means were resorted to, in exciting the slaves. Indeed none of the slaves were engaged in any criminal enterprise; and though Allen supposed that the meeting at Joe's house, between Scott and himself, was one designed by the Negroes for purposes of treason, yet, in point of fact, he was mistaken. That meeting, (as far as the slaves were concerned,) was innocent, and the same remark is applicable to the meeting at Garden's house. Allen was morally, though not legally guilty. It is worthy of the consideration of the Legislature, however, whether white persons ought not to be put on the same footing as slaves, with respect to the punishment for insurrection. The Law, perhaps, ought in all cases to be, that "if any person shall raise an insurrection, or attempt to raise an insurrection, he shall suffer death."

EXTRACTS

The following extracts from a Publication in the City Gazette of the 27th of September last, under the Signature of "A South Carolinian;" are thought interesting, and appropriate, and have been therefore added.

In the Spanish conspiracy against Venice which partakes the character of this, three hundred and fifty were put to death. George II. executed fifty-four of the first men in Britain for the rebellion of 1745. Nor are we without domestic precedents. An insurrection occurred in the city of New York in 1712. As soon as the alarm-gun was fired and a detachment of the Guards appeared, the insurgents fled to the woods—there they were surrounded, several through desperation shot themselves, the rest were captured, and nineteen executed.

"Another was meditated in 1741, when there were two thousand Negroes and twelve thousand whites in the city of New York. It was then found necessary to burn thirteen and to hang eighteen Negroes with four whites; to transport eighty Negroes and five whites.

	IN NEW YORK	IN CHARLESTON
Executed,	35	35
Transported,	85	37
	120	72

"Now, a short period before the Negro plot was discovered in New York, an insurrection broke out in Carolina. Many of the ringleaders were shot or hanged, but none punished in any other mode.

"Schemes of insurrection, such as the present, cannot succeed. The white population of each state alone is adequate to suppress them. From the first settlement of Carolina, we have been accustomed to these abortive efforts. Under our proprietary government there was a notorious outlaw by the name of Sebastian; Governor Gibbes issued his proclamation, and the Indians soon entitled themselves to the reward.

"In 1730, a plan was conceived against Charleston. They (the Negroes) were allowed to assemble, were then taken, and proper examples made. Some years afterwards, what we denominate the Gullah War, occurred. This was more general—in St. Paul's Parish they appeared in arms; the greater part were killed, and not more than two or three escaped. In St. John's Parish they were discovered by Major Cordes' faithful driver Peter, and in Charleston, they were also discovered, suppressed, and punished. The Negro law of 1740, was enacted in consequence of the last, and has proved our security from that period, notwithstanding the occasional effervescences of insubordination. The history of South Carolina, in this particular, has been the history of every State in the Union.

"Another impediment to the progress of conspiracy will ever be found in the fidelity of some of our Negroes. The servant who is false to his master, would be false to his God. One act of perfidy, is but the first step in the road of corruption and of baseness, and those who on this occasion, have proved ungrateful to their owners, have also been hypocrites in religion. But it is a reputable truth, that on every such occasion, servants have been found who were worthy the kindness and confidence of their masters. "Besides, when the moment of trial comes, among large bodies of men, some will tremble, some will be shocked at what they are about to perpetrate, and others will remember that by disclosure, may be obtained more than they seek through perils. Jaffier saved Venice, and most conspiracies own men inferior to Jaffier. We must also remember that the majority of mankind would avoid dangerous enterprises. Therefore, the great body of these people, would prefer safety and quiet with their present comforts, to a hazardous commotion with an issue so fearful as it always has been, and ever will be.

"Superadded to these intrinsic securities, we have the proportion of *two* to *one* in the aggregate population of States situated like ourselves. Our sister and neighbor Tennessee has four to one, and the heroes of Orleans have but to know that we are in danger, to be with us at the first tap of the drum.

"The National Government also can preserve the peace of the country. It was established expressly to ensure domestic tranquility and suppress insurrection. It has been tried, and found efficient. The President may summon upwards of five to one. The old French government with 3,000 regulars, protected their largest colony, and a small military force is found adequate in the British West Indies. Surely the American government could, and would do as much, were it necessary. A change cannot then be effected by force, nor would it be beneficial to the United States. Our roads would swarm with paupers, and every wood be infested with bandits. But, under the existing regulations they contribute to general wealth, and are preserved from want, misery and crime."

POSTSCRIPT.

Since these sheets have been put to press, it affords him, who has been engaged in their preparation, much gratification to be able to correct one mistake, as it places the fidelity of the slave who first gave the intelligence of the intended insurrection, on much higher ground. On conferring with his master and the free man of color, whose advice he sought, it appears that the slave in question communicated the conversation at the market to his young master, before he consulted his friend (the free man of color,) and that the advice of the latter was that as "his young master was a youth, that it would be best for him immediately, without delay, to tell his mistress, that his master might receive the information the instant he came to town." (See p. 34.)

NOTES

1. That part of this section altered by A. A. 17th May, 1751, which is in brackets.

2. "Behold the day of the Lord cometh, and thy spoil shall be divided in the midst of thee. For I will gather all nations against Jerusalem to battle; and the city shall be taken, and the women ravished; and half of the city shall go forth into captivity; and the residue of the people shall not be cut off from the city. Then shall the Lord go forth, and fight against those nations, as when he fought in the day of battle."

3. "And they utterly destroyed all that was in the city, both man and woman, young and old, and ox, and sheep, and ass, with the edge of the sword."

4. As far back as the year 1809, several hundred pamphlets of an insurrectionary character were brought to Charleston, in the ship *Minerva,* from New York, by her steward, who was a black man. A citizen of Charleston, a passenger on board, immediately on her arrival informed the Intendant of the circumstance, who promptly repaired, with the City Marshal, to the vessel; but did not arrive there in time to seize them before they were landed. The Steward was, however, committed to prison for trial, and a few of the pamphlets having been procured, he would have been tried for

his life had he not entered into an arrangement with the civil authorities of the city to leave the state, never to return therein; and what is a little remarkable, his counsel on that occasion was one of the presiding magistrates of the late court.

5. A part of the suburbs of Charleston.

6. St. Luke 11:23.

7. Monday never acknowledged to the Court that he had written two letters to Santo Domingo, but said that Vesey had, and that he in company with Peirault had carried them on board a vessel there bound.

8. The following sketch of his life is copied from the account of the intended insurrection published by the authority of the Corporation of Charleston.

"As Denmark Vesey has occupied so large a place in the conspiracy, a brief notice of him will, perhaps, be not devoid of interest. The following anecdote will show how near he was to the chance of being distinguished in the bloody events of Santo Domingo. During the revolutionary war, Captain Vesey, now an old resident of this city, commanded a ship that traded between St. Thomas' and Cape Francais (Santo Domingo). He was engaged in supplying the French of that Island with slaves. In the year 1781, he took on board at St. Thomas 390 slaves and sailed for the Cape; on the passage, he and his officers were struck with the beauty, alertness, and intelligence of a boy about fourteen years of age, whom they made a pet of, by taking him into the cabin, changing his apparel, and calling him by way of distinction *Telemaque* (which appellation has since, by gradual corruption, among the Negroes, been changed to *Denmark,* or sometimes *Telmak*). On the arrival, however, of the ship at the Cape, Captain Vesey, having no use for the boy, sold him among his other slaves, and returned to St. Thomas. On his next voyage to the Cape, he was surprised to learn from his consignee that Telemaque would be returned on his hands, as the planter, who had purchased him, represented him unsound, and subject to epileptic fits. According to the custom of trade in that place, the boy was placed in the hands of the king's physician, who decided that he was unsound, and Captain Vesey was compelled to take him back, of which he had no occasion to repent, as Denmark proved, for twenty years a most faithful slave. In 1800, Denmark drew a prize of $1,500 in the East-Bay Street Lottery, with which he purchased his freedom from his master, at six hundred dollars, much less than his real value. From that period to the day of his apprehension he has been working as a carpenter in this city, distinguished for great strength and activity. Among his color he was always looked up to with awe and respect. His temper was impetuous and domineering in the extreme, qualifying him for the despotic rule of which he was ambitious. All his passions were ungovernable and savage; and, to his numerous wives and children, he displayed the haughty and capricious cruelty of an Eastern Bashaw. He had nearly effected his escape, after information had been lodged against him. For three days the town was searched for him without success. As early as Monday, the 17th, he had concealed himself. It was not until the night of the 22d of June, during a perfect tempest, that he was found secreted in the house of one of his wives. It is to the uncommon efforts and vigilance of Mr. Wesner, and Captain Dove, of the City Guard (the latter of whom seized him), that public justice received its necessary tribute, in the execution of this man. If the party had been one moment later, he would, in all probability, have effected his escape the next day in some outward bound vessel.

9. It would be a libel on the liberality and gratitude of this community to suppose that this man can be overlooked among those who are to be rewarded for their fidelity and principle.

10. Most of the black religious communities in this place, are divided into classes, over which a Leader is placed, having the confidence of the Pastor of the Church.

11. This witness came forward voluntarily, and gave information of the intended insurrection, and of the places and those concerned, as far as his information extended, *previously* to the appointed day, and only asked that his name would not be divulged, which the Court pledged themselves to conceal as far as it depended on them. His name is therefore suppressed—*He is in no way inculpated.*

12. This witness as regards the concealment of his name, stands precisely in the same situation as No. 1.

13. Rolla on his arraignment and throughout his trial, until after the evidence closed denied his guilt, and pretended utter ignorance of the intended insurrection.

14. The mode of execution ordered in this and the subsequent cases where the convicts were sentenced to death, was the Gallows.

15. Against this witness there was no charge in relation to the insurrection—secrecy as to his name was pledged to him.

16. This witness is in the precise situation, and had the same pledge given him as No. 3.

17. Against this witness the Court had not a tittle of testimony —he consented without hesitation to become a witness, and to give all the information he possessed, a pledge having been previously given him by the Court that he should not be prosecuted or his name revealed.

18. The Court considered Jesse's confession good evidence, because it was voluntarily made under the conviction of approach-

ing death, and because the Court did not think the principle of the
common law relative to the testimony of a convicted prisoner to
be applicable to an individual in the situation of this witness.
Moreover, the confession of Jesse and Rolla to the Court were
made before conviction.

19. When this witness was about to be examined in the presence of Gullah Jack, it was not without considerable difficulty
that the Court satisfied him that he need no longer fear Jack's
conjurations, (as he called them). It was in the course of this
witness' evidence that Jack laid aside the character of the fool he
was counterfeiting, and showed his real character.

20. Publisher's Note. This material was also censored from
the first edition.

21. At the conclusion of this trial on the 13th of July, Mr.
James Legare, from feeble health and great exhaustion during the
previous sittings of the Court, asked, and obtained, leave to with-
draw; whereupon Mr. Henry Deas, was summoned by the Magistrates, who took his seat and served until the adjournment of the
Court.

22. Upon the testimony of this witness, the Court placed
great reliance. His open, frank, and blunt manner convinced
everyone who heard him that he was incapable of uttering a false-
hood, and that he possessed many fine traits of character. The following account of his life was politely furnished by his owner.
Peirault was born at Jumba in Africa, about a week's travel from
Goree. Mamadu his father, who is wealthy and owns about 60
working hands, trades to Hassou with tobacco and salt, in exchange for which he receives gold; to which place Peirault accompanied him six times. Peirault was engaged in three battles
against the people of Hassou, who do not cultivate their lands,

but make predatory incursions into the cultivated territories of their neighbors. Peirault also fought twice against the people of Darah, but in the second battle he was taken prisoner and carried to that place. Here his brother-in-law saw him, and offered to the Captain of a Brig three slaves for him if he would wait his return from Jumba. The Captain, however, could not delay his voyage, and Peirault was brought to Charleston in a Brig belonging to Mr. Delaire, who kept him for his own service. In 1814, he was purchased by his present owner, who is satisfied with his conduct since he bought him. His master stated that he is very tenacious, whenever he conceives that he is right, and that he believes he would rather suffer death than deviate from the truth—that those who are not accustomed to his mode of expressing himself would be affronted by his bluntness, but that he does not mean to offend.

23. Lot denied Jesse's accusations, and as no one at that time but Jesse accused him, against whom Lot volunteered his evidence and was principally instrumental in his conviction, the Court dismissed Lot. After Monday, Jack (Purcell) and Frank had been arrested, however, Lot (fearing they would inculpate him), absconded, and was arrested through the vigilance and activity of several gentlemen, who plant in St. James' Santee, as he was attempting to effect his escape across by Libben's Ferry, for the purpose (it is supposed) of getting beyond the limits of the State.

24. It was reported that Mrs. Fick said that Scipio had left a sword and pistol with her to keep for him.

25. The name of the blind man had never before been mentioned in the course of these trials, and when he was brought before the Court he exhibited great perturbation. The question put to him by the Court seemed to imply a fear that he was actually on trial for his life, and it is probable if it had been deemed advisable to investigate his character and conduct, that he would have been found deeply concerned in the conspiracy. It appeared

that some of the conspirators were in the habit of resorting to his house, that he was a preacher, said to have been born with *a caul,* and was supposed to foresee events. His influence over the minds of his followers was no doubt therefore very considerable. It is probable that the timid and the wavering were brought to this High Priest of sedition, to be confirmed in good resolutions. This would account for the address to Garner about his "looking frightened," and would then show how applicable the text was "let not thy heart be troubled, neither be afraid." Peter Poyas perhaps had intimated to the Seer that Garner was timid, and hence the remark and the quotation. His own account of the affair, however, was somewhat different. He said he possessed a Gift—a species of second sight—which came to him after prayer or in dreams. That the insurrection had never been mentioned to him, but that he had foreseen something of that sort, and therefore had advised his visitors, on one occasion (as he was proved to have done) "to give up the business," and had told them as a dissuasive "that the white people could fire five times while they fired once." Thus seeing Garner's timid looks—he resolved (to use his own words) to comfort him with some Scriptures.

26. Tried by the last Court.

27. Tried by the last Court.

28. Tried by the last Court.

29. The individual named by Allen, was known in this city. He was certainly well qualified on the score of courage and talent, for any desperate enterprise; no reason exists, however, to suppose that he would have engaged in one of a criminal nature.

INDEX